FREE Study Skills DVD Offer

Dear Customer,

Thank you for your purchase from Mometrix! We consider it an honor and a privilege that you have purchased our product and we want to ensure your satisfaction.

As a way of showing our appreciation and to help us better serve you, we have developed a Study Skills DVD that we would like to give you for <u>FREE</u>. This DVD covers our *best practices* for getting ready for your exam, from how to use our study materials to how to best prepare for the day of the test.

All that we ask is that you email us with feedback that would describe your experience so far with our product. Good, bad, or indifferent, we want to know what you think!

To get your FREE Study Skills DVD, email <u>freedvd@mometrix.com</u> with *FREE STUDY SKILLS DVD* in the subject line and the following information in the body of the email:

- The name of the product you purchased.
- Your product rating on a scale of 1-5, with 5 being the highest rating.
- Your feedback. It can be long, short, or anything in between. We just want to know your impressions and experience so far with our product. (Good feedback might include how our study material met your needs and ways we might be able to make it even better. You could highlight features that you found helpful or features that you think we should add.)
- Your full name and shipping address where you would like us to send your free DVD.

If you have any questions or concerns, please don't hesitate to contact me directly.

Thanks again!

Sincerely,

Jay Willis
Vice President
<u>jay.willis@mometrix.com</u>
1-800-673-8175

PERT

Exam Study Guide 2020 and 2021

PERT Test Prep Secrets

Full-Length Practice Test

Step-by-Step Review
Video Tutorials

DEAR FUTURE EXAM SUCCESS STORY

First of all, **THANK YOU** for purchasing Mometrix study materials!

Second, congratulations! You are one of the few determined test-takers who are committed to doing whatever it takes to excel on your exam. **You have come to the right place.** We developed these study materials with one goal in mind: to deliver you the information you need in a format that's concise and easy to use.

In addition to optimizing your guide for the content of the test, we've outlined our recommended steps for breaking down the preparation process into small, attainable goals so you can make sure you stay on track.

We've also analyzed the entire test-taking process, identifying the most common pitfalls and showing how you can overcome them and be ready for any curveball the test throws you.

Standardized testing is one of the biggest obstacles on your road to success, which only increases the importance of doing well in the high-pressure, high-stakes environment of test day. Your results on this test could have a significant impact on your future, and this guide provides the information and practical advice to help you achieve your full potential on test day.

Your success is our success

We would love to hear from you! If you would like to share the story of your exam success or if you have any questions or comments in regard to our products, please contact us at **800-673-8175** or **support@mometrix.com**.

Thanks again for your business and we wish you continued success!

Sincerely,
The Mometrix Test Preparation Team

TABLE OF CONTENTS

Introduction

Thank you for purchasing this resource! You have made the choice to prepare yourself for a test that could have a huge impact on your future, and this guide is designed to help you be fully ready for test day. Obviously, it's important to have a solid understanding of the test material, but you also need to be prepared for the unique environment and stressors of the test, so that you can perform to the best of your abilities.

For this purpose, the first section that appears in this guide is the **Secret Keys**. We've devoted countless hours to meticulously researching what works and what doesn't, and we've boiled down our findings to the four most impactful steps you can take to improve your performance on the test. We start at the beginning with study planning and move through the preparation process, all the way to the testing strategies that will help you get the most out of what you know when you're finally sitting in front of the test.

We recommend that you start preparing for your test as far in advance as possible. However, if you've bought this guide as a last-minute study resource and only have a few days before your test, we recommend that you skip over the first two Secret Keys since they address a long-term study plan.

If you struggle with **test anxiety**, we strongly encourage you to check out our recommendations for how you can overcome it. Test anxiety is a formidable foe, but it can be beaten, and we want to make sure you have the tools you need to defeat it.

Secret Key #1 – Plan Big, Study Small

There's a lot riding on your performance. If you want to ace this test, you're going to need to keep your skills sharp and the material fresh in your mind. You need a plan that lets you review everything you need to know while still fitting in your schedule. We'll break this strategy down into three categories.

Information Organization

Start with the information you already have: the official test outline. From this, you can make a complete list of all the concepts you need to cover before the test. Organize these concepts into groups that can be studied together, and create a list of any related vocabulary you need to learn so you can brush up on any difficult terms. You'll want to keep this vocabulary list handy once you actually start studying since you may need to add to it along the way.

Time Management

Once you have your set of study concepts, decide how to spread them out over the time you have left before the test. Break your study plan into small, clear goals so you have a manageable task for each day and know exactly what you're doing. Then just focus on one small step at a time. When you manage your time this way, you don't need to spend hours at a time studying. Studying a small block of content for a short period each day helps you retain information better and avoid stressing over how much you have left to do. You can relax knowing that you have a plan to cover everything in time. In order for this strategy to be effective though, you have to start studying early and stick to your schedule. Avoid the exhaustion and futility that comes from last-minute cramming!

Study Environment

The environment you study in has a big impact on your learning. Studying in a coffee shop, while probably more enjoyable, is not likely to be as fruitful as studying in a quiet room. It's important to keep distractions to a minimum. You're only planning to study for a short block of time, so make the most of it. Don't pause to check your phone or get up to find a snack. It's also important to **avoid multitasking**. Research has consistently shown that multitasking will make your studying dramatically less effective. Your study area should also be comfortable and well-lit so you don't have the distraction of straining your eyes or sitting on an uncomfortable chair.

The time of day you study is also important. You want to be rested and alert. Don't wait until just before bedtime. Study when you'll be most likely to comprehend and remember. Even better, if you know what time of day your test will be, set that time aside for study. That way your brain will be used to working on that subject at that specific time and you'll have a better chance of recalling information.

Finally, it can be helpful to team up with others who are studying for the same test. Your actual studying should be done in as isolated an environment as possible, but the work of organizing the information and setting up the study plan can be divided up. In between study sessions, you can discuss with your teammates the concepts that you're all studying and quiz each other on the details. Just be sure that your teammates are as serious about the test as you are. If you find that your study time is being replaced with social time, you might need to find a new team.

Secret Key #2 – Make Your Studying Count

You're devoting a lot of time and effort to preparing for this test, so you want to be absolutely certain it will pay off. This means doing more than just reading the content and hoping you can remember it on test day. It's important to make every minute of study count. There are two main areas you can focus on to make your studying count:

Retention

It doesn't matter how much time you study if you can't remember the material. You need to make sure you are retaining the concepts. To check your retention of the information you're learning, try recalling it at later times with minimal prompting. Try carrying around flashcards and glance at one or two from time to time or ask a friend who's also studying for the test to quiz you.

To enhance your retention, look for ways to put the information into practice so that you can apply it rather than simply recalling it. If you're using the information in practical ways, it will be much easier to remember. Similarly, it helps to solidify a concept in your mind if you're not only reading it to yourself but also explaining it to someone else. Ask a friend to let you teach them about a concept you're a little shaky on (or speak aloud to an imaginary audience if necessary). As you try to summarize, define, give examples, and answer your friend's questions, you'll understand the concepts better and they will stay with you longer. Finally, step back for a big picture view and ask yourself how each piece of information fits with the whole subject. When you link the different concepts together and see them working together as a whole, it's easier to remember the individual components.

Finally, practice showing your work on any multi-step problems, even if you're just studying. Writing out each step you take to solve a problem will help solidify the process in your mind, and you'll be more likely to remember it during the test.

Modality

Modality simply refers to the means or method by which you study. Choosing a study modality that fits your own individual learning style is crucial. No two people learn best in exactly the same way, so it's important to know your strengths and use them to your advantage.

For example, if you learn best by visualization, focus on visualizing a concept in your mind and draw an image or a diagram. Try color-coding your notes, illustrating them, or creating symbols that will trigger your mind to recall a learned concept. If you learn best by hearing or discussing information, find a study partner who learns the same way or read aloud to yourself. Think about how to put the information in your own words. Imagine that you are giving a lecture on the topic and record yourself so you can listen to it later.

For any learning style, flashcards can be helpful. Organize the information so you can take advantage of spare moments to review. Underline key words or phrases. Use different colors for different categories. Mnemonic devices (such as creating a short list in which every item starts with the same letter) can also help with retention. Find what works best for you and use it to store the information in your mind most effectively and easily.

3

Secret Key #3 – Practice the Right Way

Your success on test day depends not only on how many hours you put into preparing, but also on whether you prepared the right way. It's good to check along the way to see if your studying is paying off. One of the most effective ways to do this is by taking practice tests to evaluate your progress. Practice tests are useful because they show exactly where you need to improve. Every time you take a practice test, pay special attention to these three groups of questions:

- The questions you got wrong
- The questions you had to guess on, even if you guessed right
- The questions you found difficult or slow to work through

This will show you exactly what your weak areas are, and where you need to devote more study time. Ask yourself why each of these questions gave you trouble. Was it because you didn't understand the material? Was it because you didn't remember the vocabulary? Do you need more repetitions on this type of question to build speed and confidence? Dig into those questions and figure out how you can strengthen your weak areas as you go back to review the material.

Additionally, many practice tests have a section explaining the answer choices. It can be tempting to read the explanation and think that you now have a good understanding of the concept. However, an explanation likely only covers part of the question's broader context. Even if the explanation makes sense, **go back and investigate** every concept related to the question until you're positive you have a thorough understanding.

As you go along, keep in mind that the practice test is just that: practice. Memorizing these questions and answers will not be very helpful on the actual test because it is unlikely to have any of the same exact questions. If you only know the right answers to the sample questions, you won't be prepared for the real thing. **Study the concepts** until you understand them fully, and then you'll be able to answer any question that shows up on the test.

It's important to wait on the practice tests until you're ready. If you take a test on your first day of study, you may be overwhelmed by the amount of material covered and how much you need to learn. Work up to it gradually.

On test day, you'll need to be prepared for answering questions, managing your time, and using the test-taking strategies you've learned. It's a lot to balance, like a mental marathon that will have a big impact on your future. Like training for a marathon, you'll need to start slowly and work your way up. When test day arrives, you'll be ready.

Start with the strategies you've read in the first two Secret Keys—plan your course and study in the way that works best for you. If you have time, consider using multiple study resources to get different approaches to the same concepts. It can be helpful to see difficult concepts from more than one angle. Then find a good source for practice tests. Many times, the test website will suggest potential study resources or provide sample tests.

Secret Key #4 – Have a Plan for Guessing

When you're taking the test, you may find yourself stuck on a question. Some of the answer choices seem better than others, but you don't see the one answer choice that is obviously correct. What do you do?

The scenario described above is very common, yet most test takers have not effectively prepared for it. Developing and practicing a plan for guessing may be one of the single most effective uses of your time as you get ready for the exam.

In developing your plan for guessing, there are three questions to address:

- When should you start the guessing process?
- How should you narrow down the choices?
- Which answer should you choose?

When to Start the Guessing Process

Unless your plan for guessing is to select C every time (which, despite its merits, is not what we recommend), you need to leave yourself enough time to apply your answer elimination strategies. Since you have a limited amount of time for each question, that means that if you're going to give yourself the best shot at guessing correctly, you have to decide quickly whether or not you will guess.

Of course, the best-case scenario is that you don't have to guess at all, so first, see if you can answer the question based on your knowledge of the subject and basic reasoning skills. Focus on the key words in the question and try to jog your memory of related topics. Give yourself a chance to bring the knowledge to mind, but once you realize that you don't have (or you can't access) the knowledge you need to answer the question, it's time to start the guessing process.

It's almost always better to start the guessing process too early than too late. It only takes a few seconds to remember something and answer the question from knowledge. Carefully eliminating wrong answer choices takes longer. Plus, going through the process of eliminating answer choices can actually help jog your memory.

Summary: Start the guessing process as soon as you decide that you can't answer the question based on your knowledge.

How to Narrow Down the Choices

The next chapter in this book (**Test-Taking Strategies**) includes a wide range of strategies for how to approach questions and how to look for answer choices to eliminate. You will definitely want to read those carefully, practice them, and figure out which ones work best for you. Here though, we're going to address a mindset rather than a particular strategy.

Your chances of guessing an answer correctly depend on how many options you are choosing from.

How many choices you have	How likely you are to guess correctly
5	20%
4	25%
3	33%
2	50%
1	100%

You can see from this chart just how valuable it is to be able to eliminate incorrect answers and make an educated guess, but there are two things that many test takers do that cause them to miss out on the benefits of guessing:

- Accidentally eliminating the correct answer
- Selecting an answer based on an impression

We'll look at the first one here, and the second one in the next section.

To avoid accidentally eliminating the correct answer, we recommend a thought exercise called **the $5 challenge**. In this challenge, you only eliminate an answer choice from contention if you are willing to bet $5 on it being wrong. Why $5? Five dollars is a small but not insignificant amount of money. It's an amount you could afford to lose but wouldn't want to throw away. And while losing $5 once might not hurt too much, doing it twenty times will set you back $100. In the same way, each small decision you make—eliminating a choice here, guessing on a question there—won't by itself impact your score very much, but when you put them all together, they can make a big difference. By holding each answer choice elimination decision to a higher standard, you can reduce the risk of accidentally eliminating the correct answer.

The $5 challenge can also be applied in a positive sense: If you are willing to bet $5 that an answer choice *is* correct, go ahead and mark it as correct.

Summary: Only eliminate an answer choice if you are willing to bet $5 that it is wrong.

6

Which Answer to Choose

You're taking the test. You've run into a hard question and decided you'll have to guess. You've eliminated all the answer choices you're willing to bet $5 on. Now you have to pick an answer. Why do we even need to talk about this? Why can't you just pick whichever one you feel like when the time comes?

The answer to these questions is that if you don't come into the test with a plan, you'll rely on your impression to select an answer choice, and if you do that, you risk falling into a trap. The test writers know that everyone who takes their test will be guessing on some of the questions, so they intentionally write wrong answer choices to seem plausible. You still have to pick an answer though, and if the wrong answer choices are designed to look right, how can you ever be sure that you're not falling for their trap? The best solution we've found to this dilemma is to take the decision out of your hands entirely. Here is the process we recommend:

Once you've eliminated any choices that you are confident (willing to bet $5) are wrong, select the first remaining choice as your answer.

Whether you choose to select the first remaining choice, the second, or the last, the important thing is that you use some preselected standard. Using this approach guarantees that you will not be enticed into selecting an answer choice that looks right, because you are not basing your decision on how the answer choices look.

This is not meant to make you question your knowledge. Instead, it is to help you recognize the difference between your knowledge and your impressions. There's a huge difference between thinking an answer is right because of what you know, and thinking an answer is right because it looks or sounds like it should be right.

Summary: To ensure that your selection is appropriately random, make a predetermined selection from among all answer choices you have not eliminated.

Test-Taking Strategies

This section contains a list of test-taking strategies that you may find helpful as you work through the test. By taking what you know and applying logical thought, you can maximize your chances of answering any question correctly!

It is very important to realize that every question is different and every person is different: no single strategy will work on every question, and no single strategy will work for every person. That's why we've included all of them here, so you can try them out and determine which ones work best for different types of questions and which ones work best for you.

Question Strategies

READ CAREFULLY

Read the question and answer choices carefully. Don't miss the question because you misread the terms. You have plenty of time to read each question thoroughly and make sure you understand what is being asked. Yet a happy medium must be attained, so don't waste too much time. You must read carefully, but efficiently.

CONTEXTUAL CLUES

Look for contextual clues. If the question includes a word you are not familiar with, look at the immediate context for some indication of what the word might mean. Contextual clues can often give you all the information you need to decipher the meaning of an unfamiliar word. Even if you can't determine the meaning, you may be able to narrow down the possibilities enough to make a solid guess at the answer to the question.

PREFIXES

If you're having trouble with a word in the question or answer choices, try dissecting it. Take advantage of every clue that the word might include. Prefixes and suffixes can be a huge help. Usually they allow you to determine a basic meaning. Pre- means before, post- means after, pro - is positive, de- is negative. From prefixes and suffixes, you can get an idea of the general meaning of the word and try to put it into context.

HEDGE WORDS

Watch out for critical hedge words, such as *likely, may, can, sometimes, often, almost, mostly, usually, generally, rarely,* and *sometimes.* Question writers insert these hedge phrases to cover every possibility. Often an answer choice will be wrong simply because it leaves no room for exception. Be on guard for answer choices that have definitive words such as *exactly* and *always.*

SWITCHBACK WORDS

Stay alert for *switchbacks.* These are the words and phrases frequently used to alert you to shifts in thought. The most common switchback words are *but, although,* and *however.* Others include *nevertheless, on the other hand, even though, while, in spite of, despite, regardless of.* Switchback words are important to catch because they can change the direction of the question or an answer choice.

8

FACE VALUE

When in doubt, use common sense. Accept the situation in the problem at face value. Don't read too much into it. These problems will not require you to make wild assumptions. If you have to go beyond creativity and warp time or space in order to have an answer choice fit the question, then you should move on and consider the other answer choices. These are normal problems rooted in reality. The applicable relationship or explanation may not be readily apparent, but it is there for you to figure out. Use your common sense to interpret anything that isn't clear.

Answer Choice Strategies

ANSWER SELECTION

The most thorough way to pick an answer choice is to identify and eliminate wrong answers until only one is left, then confirm it is the correct answer. Sometimes an answer choice may immediately seem right, but be careful. The test writers will usually put more than one reasonable answer choice on each question, so take a second to read all of them and make sure that the other choices are not equally obvious. As long as you have time left, it is better to read every answer choice than to pick the first one that looks right without checking the others.

ANSWER CHOICE FAMILIES

An answer choice family consists of two (in rare cases, three) answer choices that are very similar in construction and cannot all be true at the same time. If you see two answer choices that are direct opposites or parallels, one of them is usually the correct answer. For instance, if one answer choice says that quantity x increases and another either says that quantity x decreases (opposite) or says that quantity y increases (parallel), then those answer choices would fall into the same family. An answer choice that doesn't match the construction of the answer choice family is more likely to be incorrect. Most questions will not have answer choice families, but when they do appear, you should be prepared to recognize them.

ELIMINATE ANSWERS

Eliminate answer choices as soon as you realize they are wrong, but make sure you consider all possibilities. If you are eliminating answer choices and realize that the last one you are left with is also wrong, don't panic. Start over and consider each choice again. There may be something you missed the first time that you will realize on the second pass.

AVOID FACT TRAPS

Don't be distracted by an answer choice that is factually true but doesn't answer the question. You are looking for the choice that answers the question. Stay focused on what the question is asking for so you don't accidentally pick an answer that is true but incorrect. Always go back to the question and make sure the answer choice you've selected actually answers the question and is not merely a true statement.

EXTREME STATEMENTS

In general, you should avoid answers that put forth extreme actions as standard practice or proclaim controversial ideas as established fact. An answer choice that states the "process should be used in certain situations, if..." is much more likely to be correct than one that states the "process should be discontinued completely." The first is a calm rational statement and doesn't even make a definitive, uncompromising stance, using a hedge word *if* to provide wiggle room, whereas the second choice is a radical idea and far more extreme.

9

BENCHMARK

As you read through the answer choices and you come across one that seems to answer the question well, mentally select that answer choice. This is not your final answer, but it's the one that will help you evaluate the other answer choices. The one that you selected is your benchmark or standard for judging each of the other answer choices. Every other answer choice must be compared to your benchmark. That choice is correct until proven otherwise by another answer choice beating it. If you find a better answer, then that one becomes your new benchmark. Once you've decided that no other choice answers the question as well as your benchmark, you have your final answer.

PREDICT THE ANSWER

Before you even start looking at the answer choices, it is often best to try to predict the answer. When you come up with the answer on your own, it is easier to avoid distractions and traps because you will know exactly what to look for. The right answer choice is unlikely to be word-for-word what you came up with, but it should be a close match. Even if you are confident that you have the right answer, you should still take the time to read each option before moving on.

General Strategies

TOUGH QUESTIONS

If you are stumped on a problem or it appears too hard or too difficult, don't waste time. Move on! Remember though, if you can quickly check for obviously incorrect answer choices, your chances of guessing correctly are greatly improved. Before you completely give up, at least try to knock out a couple of possible answers. Eliminate what you can and then guess at the remaining answer choices before moving on.

CHECK YOUR WORK

Since you will probably not know every term listed and the answer to every question, it is important that you get credit for the ones that you do know. Don't miss any questions through careless mistakes. If at all possible, try to take a second to look back over your answer selection and make sure you've selected the correct answer choice and haven't made a costly careless mistake (such as marking an answer choice that you didn't mean to mark). This quick double check should more than pay for itself in caught mistakes for the time it costs.

DON'T RUSH

It is very easy to make errors when you are in a hurry. Maintaining a fast pace in answering questions is pointless if it makes you miss questions that you would have gotten right otherwise. Test writers like to include distracting information and wrong answers that seem right. Taking a little extra time to avoid careless mistakes can make all the difference in your test score. Find a pace that allows you to be confident in the answers that you select.

KEEP MOVING

Panicking will not help you pass the test, so do your best to stay calm and keep moving. Taking deep breaths and going through the answer elimination steps you practiced can help to break through a stress barrier and keep your pace.

Final Notes

The combination of a solid foundation of content knowledge and the confidence that comes from practicing your plan for applying that knowledge is the key to maximizing your performance on test day. As your foundation of content knowledge is built up and strengthened, you'll find that the strategies included in this chapter become more and more effective in helping you quickly sift through the distractions and traps of the test to isolate the correct answer.

Now it's time to move on to the test content chapters of this book, but be sure to keep your goal in mind. As you read, think about how you will be able to apply this information on the test. If you've already seen sample questions for the test and you have an idea of the question format and style, try to come up with questions of your own that you can answer based on what you're reading. This will give you valuable practice applying your knowledge in the same ways you can expect to on test day.

Good luck and good studying!

Mathematics

Numbers and Operations

CLASSIFYING NUMBERS

There are several different kinds of numbers. When you learn to count as a child, you typically start with *Natural Numbers*. These are sometimes called "counting numbers" and begin with 1, 2, 3 ... etc. *Whole Numbers* include all natural numbers as well as 0. *Integers* include all whole numbers as well as their associated negative values (...-2, -1, 0, 1, 2...). Fractions with an integer in the numerator and a non-zero integer in the denominator are called *Rational Numbers*. Numbers such as π, that are non-terminating and non-repeating and cannot be expressed as a fraction, are considered *Irrational Numbers*. Any number that contains the imaginary number i, where $i^2 = -1$ and $i = \sqrt{-1}$, is referred to as a *Complex Number*. All natural numbers, whole numbers, integers, rational numbers, and irrational numbers are *Real Numbers*; complex numbers are not real numbers.

Aside from the number 1, all natural numbers can either be classified as prime or composite. *Prime Numbers* are natural numbers greater than 1 whose only factors are 1 and itself. On the other hand, *Composite Numbers* are natural numbers greater than 1 that are not prime numbers. 1 is a special case in that it is neither a prime number nor composite number. According to the *Fundamental Theorem of Arithmetic*, every composite number can be uniquely written as the product of prime numbers.

Numbers are the basic building blocks of mathematics. Specific features of numbers are identified by the following terms:

Integers – The set of positive and negative numbers, including zero. Integers do not include fractions $\left(\frac{1}{3}\right)$, decimals (0.56), or mixed numbers $\left(7\frac{3}{4}\right)$.

Even number – Any integer that can be divided by 2 without leaving a remainder. For example: 2, 4, 6, 8, and so on.

Odd number – Any integer that cannot be divided evenly by 2. For example: 3, 5, 7, 9, and so on.

Decimal number – a number that uses a decimal point to show the part of the number that is less than one. Example: 1.234.

Decimal point – a symbol used to separate the ones place from the tenths place in decimals or dollars from cents in currency.

Decimal place – the position of a number to the right of the decimal point. In the decimal 0.123, the 1 is in the first place to the right of the decimal point, indicating tenths; the 2 is in the second place, indicating hundredths; and the 3 is in the third place, indicating thousandths.

The decimal, or base 10, system is a number system that uses ten different digits (0, 1, 2, 3, 4, 5, 6, 7, 8, 9). An example of a number system that uses something other than ten digits is the binary, or

13

base 2, number system, used by computers, which uses only the numbers 0 and 1. It is thought that the decimal system originated because people had only their 10 fingers for counting.

FRACTIONS

A fraction is a number that is expressed as one integer written above another integer, with a dividing line between them $\left(\frac{x}{y}\right)$. It represents the quotient of the two numbers "x divided by y." It can also be thought of as x out of y equal parts. The top number of a fraction is called the numerator, and it represents the number of parts under consideration. The 1 in $\frac{1}{4}$ means that 1 part out of the whole is being considered in the calculation. The bottom number of a fraction is called the denominator, and it represents the total number of equal parts. The 4 in $\frac{1}{4}$ means that the whole consists of 4 equal parts. A fraction cannot have a denominator of zero; this is referred to as "undefined."

Fractions can be manipulated by multiplying or dividing (but not adding or subtracting) both the numerator and denominator by the same number, without changing the value of the fraction. If you divide both numbers by a common factor, you are reducing or simplifying the fraction. Two fractions that have the same value, but are expressed differently are known as equivalent fractions. For example, $\frac{2}{10}, \frac{3}{15}, \frac{4}{20}$, and $\frac{5}{25}$ are all equivalent fractions. They can also all be reduced or simplified to $\frac{1}{5}$.

When two fractions are manipulated so that they have the same denominator, this is known as finding a common denominator. The number chosen to be that common denominator should be the least common multiple of the two original denominators. Example: $\frac{3}{4}$ and $\frac{5}{6}$; the least common multiple of 4 and 6 is 12. Manipulating to achieve the common denominator: $\frac{3}{4} = \frac{9}{12}; \frac{5}{6} = \frac{10}{12}$.

A fraction whose denominator is greater than its numerator is known as a proper fraction, while a fraction whose numerator is greater than its denominator is known as an improper fraction. Proper fractions have values less than one and improper fractions have values greater than one.

MIXED NUMBERS AND COMPLEX FRACTIONS

A mixed number is a number that contains both an integer and a fraction. Any improper fraction can be rewritten as a mixed number. Example: $\frac{8}{3} = \frac{6}{3} + \frac{2}{3} = 2 + \frac{2}{3} = 2\frac{2}{3}$. Similarly, any mixed number can be rewritten as an improper fraction. Example: $1\frac{3}{5} = 1 + \frac{3}{5} = \frac{5}{5} + \frac{3}{5} = \frac{8}{5}$.

A fraction that contains a fraction in the numerator, denominator, or both is called a *Complex Fraction*. These can be solved in a number of ways; with the simplest being by following the order of operations as stated earlier. For example, $\left(\frac{4}{7}\right) \Big/ \left(\frac{5}{8}\right) = 0.571 \big/ 0.625 = 0.914$. Another way to solve

this problem is to multiply the fraction in the numerator by the reciprical of the fraction in the denominator. For example, $\dfrac{\left(\frac{4}{7}\right)}{\left(\frac{5}{8}\right)} = \dfrac{4}{7} \times \dfrac{8}{5} = \dfrac{32}{35} = 0.914.$

Review Video: <u>Fractions</u>
Visit mometrix.com/academy and enter code: 262335

DECIMALS

DECIMAL ILLUSTRATION

Use a model to represent the decimal: 0.24. Write 0.24 as a fraction.

The decimal 0.24 is twenty-four hundredths. One possible model to represent this fraction is to draw 100 pennies, since each penny is worth 1 one hundredth of a dollar. Draw one hundred circles to represent one hundred pennies. Shade 24 of the pennies to represent the decimal twenty-four hundredths.

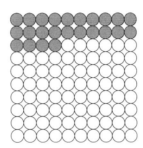

To write the decimal as a fraction, write a fraction: $\dfrac{\text{\# shaded spaces}}{\text{\# total spaces}}$. The number of shaded spaces is 24, and the total number of spaces is 100, so as a fraction 0.24 equals $\dfrac{24}{100}$. This fraction can then be reduced to $\dfrac{6}{25}$.

OPERATIONS

There are four basic mathematical operations:

Addition increases the value of one quantity by the value of another quantity. Example: 2 + 4 = 6; 8 + 9 = 17. The result is called the sum. With addition, the order does not matter. 4 + 2 = 2 + 4.

Subtraction is the opposite operation to addition; it decreases the value of one quantity by the value of another quantity. Example: 6 – 4 = 2; 17 – 8 = 9. The result is called the difference. Note that with subtraction, the order does matter. 6 – 4 ≠ 4 – 6.

Multiplication can be thought of as repeated addition. One number tells how many times to add the other number to itself. Example: 3 × 2 (three times two) = 2 + 2 + 2 = 6. With multiplication, the order does not matter. 2 × 3 (or 3 + 3) = 3 × 2 (or 2 + 2 + 2).

Division is the opposite operation to multiplication; one number tells us how many parts to divide the other number into. Example: 20 ÷ 4 = 5; if 20 is split into 4 equal parts, each part is 5. With division, the order of the numbers does matter. 20 ÷ 4 ≠ 4 ÷ 20.

PARENTHESES

Parentheses are used to designate which operations should be done first when there are multiple operations. Example: 4 – (2 + 1) = 1; the parentheses tell us that we must add 2 and 1, and then subtract the sum from 4, rather than subtracting 2 from 4 and then adding 1 (this would give us an answer of 3).

EXPONENT

An exponent is a superscript number placed next to another number at the top right. It indicates how many times the base number is to be multiplied by itself. Exponents provide a shorthand way to write what would be a longer mathematical expression. Example: $a^2 = a \times a$; $2^4 = 2 \times 2 \times 2 \times 2$. A number with an exponent of 2 is said to be "squared," while a number with an exponent of 3 is said to be "cubed." The value of a number raised to an exponent is called its power. So, 8^4 is read as "8 to the 4th power," or "8 raised to the power of 4." A negative exponent is the same as the reciprocal of a positive exponent. Example: $a^{-2} = 1/a^2$.

ORDER OF OPERATIONS

Order of Operations is a set of rules that dictates the order in which we must perform each operation in an expression so that we will evaluate it accurately. If we have an expression that includes multiple different operations, Order of Operations tells us which operations to do first. The most common mnemonic for Order of Operations is PEMDAS, or "Please Excuse My Dear Aunt Sally." PEMDAS stands for Parentheses, Exponents, Multiplication, Division, Addition, Subtraction. It is important to understand that multiplication and division have equal precedence, as do addition and subtraction, so those pairs of operations are simply worked from left to right in order.

Example: Evaluate the expression $5 + 20 \div 4 \times (2 + 3)^2 - 6$ using the correct order of operations.

P: Perform the operations inside the parentheses, (2 + 3) = 5.

E: Simplify the exponents, $(5)^2 = 25$.

The equation now looks like this: $5 + 20 \div 4 \times 25 - 6$.

MD: Perform multiplication and division from left to right, 20 ÷ 4 = 5; then 5 × 25 = 125.

The equation now looks like this: 5 + 125 – 6.

AS: Perform addition and subtraction from left to right, 5 + 125 = 130; then 130 – 6 = 124.

> **Review Video: Order of Operations**
> Visit mometrix.com/academy and enter code: 259675

LAW OF EXPONENTS

The laws of exponents are as follows:

1. Any number to the power of 1 is equal to itself: $a^1 = a$.
2. The number 1 raised to any power is equal to 1: $1^n = 1$.
3. Any number raised to the power of 0 is equal to 1: $a^0 = 1$.
4. Add exponents to multiply powers of the same base number: $a^n \times a^m = a^{n+m}$.
5. Subtract exponents to divide powers of the same number; that is $a^n \div a^m = a^{n-m}$.
6. Multiply exponents to raise a power to a power: $(a^n)^m = a^{n \times m}$.

7. If multiplied or divided numbers inside parentheses are collectively raised to a power, this is the same as each individual term being raised to that power: $(a \times b)^n = a^n \times b^n$; $(a \div b)^n = a^n \div b^n$.

Note: Exponents do not have to be integers. Fractional or decimal exponents follow all the rules above as well. Example: $5^{\frac{1}{4}} \times 5^{\frac{3}{4}} = 5^{\frac{1}{4}+\frac{3}{4}} = 5^1 = 5$.

OPERATIONS WITH FRACTIONS
ADDING AND SUBTRACTING FRACTIONS

If two fractions have a common denominator, they can be added or subtracted simply by adding or subtracting the two numerators and retaining the same denominator. Example: $\frac{1}{2} + \frac{1}{4} = \frac{2}{4} + \frac{1}{4} = \frac{3}{4}$. If the two fractions do not already have the same denominator, one or both of them must be manipulated to achieve a common denominator before they can be added or subtracted.

MULTIPLYING FRACTIONS

Two fractions can be multiplied by multiplying the two numerators to find the new numerator and the two denominators to find the new denominator. Example: $\frac{1}{3} \times \frac{2}{3} = \frac{1 \times 2}{3 \times 3} = \frac{2}{9}$.

DIVIDING FRACTIONS

Two fractions can be divided by flipping the numerator and denominator of the second fraction and then proceeding as though it were a multiplication. Example: $\frac{2}{3} \div \frac{3}{4} = \frac{2}{3} \times \frac{4}{3} = \frac{8}{9}$.

OPERATIONS WITH DECIMALS
ADDING AND SUBTRACTING DECIMALS

When adding and subtracting decimals, the decimal points must always be aligned. Adding decimals is just like adding regular whole numbers. Example: 4.5 + 2 = 6.5.

If the problem-solver does not properly align the decimal points, an incorrect answer of 4.7 may result. An easy way to add decimals is to align all of the decimal points in a vertical column visually. This will allow one to see exactly where the decimal should be placed in the final answer. Begin adding from right to left. Add each column in turn, making sure to carry the number to the left if a column adds up to more than 9. The same rules apply to the subtraction of decimals.

> **Review Video: Adding and Subtracting Decimals**
> Visit mometrix.com/academy and enter code: 381101

MULTIPLYING DECIMALS

A simple multiplication problem has two components: a multiplicand and a multiplier. When multiplying decimals, work as though the numbers were whole rather than decimals. Once the final product is calculated, count the number of places to the right of the decimal in both the multiplicand and the multiplier. Then, count that number of places from the right of the product and place the decimal in that position. For example, 12.3 × 2.56 has three places to the right of the respective decimals. Multiply 123 × 256 to get 31488. Now, beginning on the right, count three places to the left and insert the decimal. The final product will be 31.488.

> **Review Video: Multiplying Decimals**
> Visit mometrix.com/academy and enter code: 731574

DIVIDING DECIMALS

Every division problem has a divisor and a dividend. The dividend is the number that is being divided. In the problem $14 \div 7$, 14 is the dividend and 7 is the divisor. In a division problem with decimals, the divisor must be converted into a whole number. Begin by moving the decimal in the divisor to the right until a whole number is created. Next, move the decimal in the dividend the same number of spaces to the right. For example, 4.9 into 24.5 would become 49 into 245. The decimal was moved one space to the right to create a whole number in the divisor, and then the same was done for the dividend. Once the whole numbers are created, the problem is carried out normally: $245 \div 49 = 5$.

> **Review Video: Dividing Decimals**
> Visit mometrix.com/academy and enter code: 560690

ABSOLUTE VALUE

A precursor to working with negative numbers is understanding what **absolute values** are. A number's absolute value is simply the distance away from zero a number is on the number line. The absolute value of a number is always positive and is written $|x|$. For example, the absolute value of 3, written as $|3|$, is 3 because the distance between 0 and 3 on a number line is three units. Likewise, the absolute value of –3, written as $|-3|$, is 3 because the distance between 0 and –3 on a number line is three units. So $|3| = |-3|$.

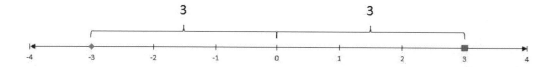

> **Review Video: Absolute Value**
> Visit mometrix.com/academy and enter code: 314669

WORKING WITH POSITIVE & NEGATIVE NUMBERS

When adding signed numbers, if the signs are the same simply add the absolute values of the addends and apply the original sign to the sum. For example, $(+4) + (+8) = +12$ and $(-4) + (-8) = -12$. When the original signs are different, take the absolute values of the addends and subtract the smaller value from the larger value, then apply the original sign of the larger value to the difference. For instance, $(+4) + (-8) = -4$ and $(-4) + (+8) = +4$.

For subtracting signed numbers, change the sign of the number after the minus symbol and then follow the same rules used for addition. For example, $(+4) - (+8) = (+4) + (-8) = -4$.

If the signs are the same the product is positive when multiplying signed numbers. For example, $(+4) \times (+8) = +32$ and $(-4) \times (-8) = +32$. If the signs are opposite, the product is negative. For example, $(+4) \times (-8) = -32$ and $(-4) \times (+8) = -32$. When more than two factors are multiplied together, the sign of the product is determined by how many negative factors are present. If there are an odd number of negative factors then the product is negative, whereas an even number of negative factors indicates a positive product. For instance, $(+4) \times (-8) \times (-2) = +64$ and $(-4) \times (-8) \times (-2) = -64$.

The rules for dividing signed numbers are similar to multiplying signed numbers. If the dividend and divisor have the same sign, the quotient is positive. If the dividend and divisor have opposite signs, the quotient is negative. For example, $(-4) \div (+8) = -0.5$.

PERCENTAGES

Percentages can be thought of as fractions that are based on a whole of 100; that is, one whole is equal to 100%. The word percent means "per hundred." Fractions can be expressed as percents by finding equivalent fractions with a denomination of 100. Example: $\frac{7}{10} = \frac{70}{100} = 70\%$; $\frac{1}{4} = \frac{25}{100} = 25\%$.

To express a percentage as a fraction, divide the percentage number by 100 and reduce the fraction to its simplest possible terms. Example: $60\% = \frac{60}{100} = \frac{3}{5}$; $96\% = \frac{96}{100} = \frac{24}{25}$.

> **Review Video: Percentages**
> Visit mometrix.com/academy and enter code: 141911

CONVERTING PERCENTS, FRACTIONS, AND DECIMALS

Converting decimals to percentages and percentages to decimals is as simple as moving the decimal point. To convert from a decimal to a percent, move the decimal point two places to the right. To convert from a percent to a decimal, move it two places to the left. Example: $0.23 = 23\%$; $5.34 = 534\%$; $0.007 = 0.7\%$; $700\% = 7.00$; $86\% = 0.86$; $0.15\% = 0.0015$.

It may be helpful to remember that the percentage number will always be larger than the equivalent decimal number.

> **Review Video: Converting Decimals to Fractions and Percentages**
> Visit mometrix.com/academy and enter code: 986765

Example 1

15% can be written as a fraction and as a decimal. 15% written as a fraction is $\frac{15}{100}$ which equals $\frac{3}{20}$. 15% written as a decimal is 0.15.

To convert a percent to a fraction, follow these steps:

1) Write the percent over 100 because percent means "per one hundred." So, 15% can be written as $\frac{15}{100}$.

2) Fractions should be written in simplest form, which means that the numbers in the numerator and denominator should be reduced if possible. Both 15 and 100 can be divided by 5.

3) Therefore, $\frac{15 \div 5}{100 \div 5} = \frac{3}{20}$.

To convert a percent to a decimal, follow these steps:

1) Write the percent over 100 because percent means "per one hundred." So, 15% can be written as $\frac{15}{100}$.

2) 15 divided by 100 equals 0.15, so 15% = 0.15. In other words, when converting from a percent to a decimal, drop the percent sign and move the decimal two places to the left.

Example 2

Write 24.36% as a fraction and then as a decimal. Explain how you made these conversions.

24.36% written as a fraction is $\frac{24.36}{100}$, or $\frac{2436}{10,000}$, which reduces to $\frac{609}{2500}$. 24.36% written as a decimal is 0.2436. Recall that dividing by 100 moves the decimal two places to the left.

> **Review Video: Converting Percentages to Decimals and Fractions**
> Visit mometrix.com/academy and enter code: 287297

Example 3

Convert $\frac{4}{5}$ to a decimal and to a percent.

To convert a fraction to a decimal, simply divide the numerator by the denominator in the fraction. The numerator is the top number in the fraction and the denominator is the bottom number in a fraction. So $\frac{4}{5} = 4 \div 5 = 0.80 = 0.8$.

Percent means "per hundred." $\frac{4 \times 20}{5 \times 20} = \frac{80}{100} = 80\%$.

Example 4

Convert $3\frac{2}{5}$ to a decimal and to a percent.

The mixed number $3\frac{2}{5}$ has a whole number and a fractional part. The fractional part $\frac{2}{5}$ can be written as a decimal by dividing 5 into 2, which gives 0.4. Adding the whole to the part gives 3.4. Alternatively, note that $3\frac{2}{5} = 3\frac{4}{10} = 3.4$

To change a decimal to a percent, multiply it by 100.
3.4(100) = 340%. Notice that this percentage is greater than 100%. This makes sense because the original mixed number $3\frac{2}{5}$ is greater than 1.

> **Review Video: Converting Fractions to Percentages and Decimals**
> Visit mometrix.com/academy and enter code: 306233

ROOTS AND PERFECT SQUARES

A root, such as a square root, is another way of writing a fractional exponent. Instead of using a superscript, roots use the radical symbol ($\sqrt{}$) to indicate the operation. A radical will have a number underneath the bar, and may sometimes have a number in the upper left: $\sqrt[n]{a}$, read as "the nth root of a." The relationship between radical notation and exponent notation can be described by this equation: $\sqrt[n]{a} = a^{1/n}$. The two special cases of n = 2 and n = 3 are called square roots and cube roots. If there is no number to the upper left, it is understood to be a square root (n = 2). Nearly all of the roots you encounter will be square roots. A square root is the same as a number raised to the

one-half power. When we say that a is the square root of b (a = $\sqrt{b}$), we mean that a multiplied by itself equals b: (a × a = b).

A perfect square is a number that has an integer for its square root. There are 10 perfect squares from 1 to 100: 1, 4, 9, 16, 25, 36, 49, 64, 81, 100 (the squares of integers 1 through 10).

FACTORS AND MULTIPLES

Factors are numbers that are multiplied together to obtain a product. For example, in the equation 2 × 3 = 6, the numbers 2 and 3 are factors. A prime number has only two factors (1 and itself), but other numbers can have many factors.

Review Video: Factors
Visit mometrix.com/academy and enter code: 920086

A common factor is a number that divides exactly into two or more other numbers. For example, the factors of 12 are 1, 2, 3, 4, 6, and 12, while the factors of 15 are 1, 3, 5, and 15. The common factors of 12 and 15 are 1 and 3. A prime factor is also a prime number. Therefore, the prime factors of 12 are 2 and 3. For 15, the prime factors are 3 and 5.

The greatest common factor (GCF) is the largest number that is a factor of two or more numbers. For example, the factors of 15 are 1, 3, 5, and 15; the factors of 35 are 1, 5, 7, and 35. Therefore, the greatest common factor of 15 and 35 is 5.

The least common multiple (LCM) is the smallest number that is a multiple of two or more numbers. For example, the multiples of 3 include 3, 6, 9, 12, 15, etc.; the multiples of 5 include 5, 10, 15, 20, etc. Therefore, the least common multiple of 3 and 5 is 15.

Review Video: Multiples
Visit mometrix.com/academy and enter code: 626738

SCIENTIFIC NOTATION

Scientific notation is a way of writing long numbers in a shorter form. The form a × 10^n is used in scientific notation. This form means that a is greater than or equal to 1 but less than 10. Also, n is the number of places the decimal must move to get from the original number to a.

Example: The number 230,400,000 is long to write. To see this value in scientific notation, place a decimal point between the first and second numbers. This includes all digits through the last non-zero digit (a = 2.304).

To find the correct power of 10, count the number of places the decimal point had to move (n = 8). The number is positive if the decimal moved to the left. Thus, the number is negative if it moved to the right. So, 230,400,000 can be written as 2.304 × 10^8.

Now, let's look at the number 0.00002304. We have the same value for a. However, this time the decimal moved 5 places to the right (n = -5). So, 0.00002304 can be written as 2.304 × 10^{-5}. This notation makes it easy to compare very large or very small numbers. By comparing exponents, you can see that 3.28 × 10^4 is smaller than 1.51 × 10^5 because 4 is less than 5.

21

ADDITION AND SUBTRACTION

To add and subtract numbers in scientific notation, you need the numbers to have the same power of 10. Next, you can add the constants. Then, you can use the power of 10 with the result.

If the constant is greater than 10 or less than 1, you need to move the decimal place. For constants less than 1, the decimal is moved to the right. For constants greater than 10, the decimal is moved to the left. Also, the power of 10 needs to change as you move the decimal place.

EXAMPLE 1

In the problem $(4.8 \times 10^4) + (2.2 \times 10^4)$, the numbers have the same power of 10. So, add 4.8 and 2.2. So, you have 7 as the result. Now, the number can be written as (7×10^4).

EXAMPLE 2

In the problem $(3.1 \times 10^8) - (2.4 \times 10^8)$, the numbers have the same power of 10. So, subtract 3.1 and 2.4, and you'll have 0.7 as the result. Remember that you cannot have a constant that is less than 1. So, you need to move the decimal place one time to the right: (7×10^8). Also, the power of 10 has to change. Now, the number can be written as (7×10^{-1}).

The power of 10 is -1 because we moved the decimal place one time to the right. Now you have $(7 \times 10^{-1}) \times 10^8$. The reason is that we still have the power of 10 as 8. Now, you can add the -1 to the +8 for an answer of (7×10^7).

EXAMPLE 3

In the problem $(5.3 \times 10^6) + (2.7 \times 10^7)$, the numbers do not have the same power of 10. So, you need one of the terms to have the same power. So, take (5.3×10^6) and change it to (0.53×10^7). Now, you can add 0.53 and 2.7. So, the number can be written as (3.23×10^7).

MULTIPLICATION

In the problem $(2.4 \times 10^3) \times (5.7 \times 10^5)$, you need to multiply 2.4 and 5.7. Then, you need to add the powers of 10 which are 3 and 5 for this example. So, you have (13.68×10^8). Remember that this cannot be an answer for scientific notation. The 13.68 for a constant is higher than 10. So, move the decimal to the left one time and change the exponent. Now, you have (1.368×10^9) as the answer.

DIVISION

In the problem $(5.6 \times 10^6) \div (2.3 \times 10^2)$, you need to divide 5.6 and 2.3. Then, you need to subtract the powers of 10 which are 6 and 2 for this example. So, you have (2.43×10^4).

Algebra

SOLVING FOR A VARIABLE

Similar to order of operation rules, algebraic rules must be obeyed to ensure a correct answer. Begin by locating all parentheses and brackets, and then solving the equations within them. Then, perform the operations necessary to remove all parentheses and brackets. Next, convert all fractions into whole numbers and combine common terms on each side of the equation. Beginning on the left side of the expression, solve operations involving multiplication and division. Then, work left to right solving operations involving addition and subtraction. Finally, cross-multiply if necessary, to reach the final solution.

EXAMPLE 1:

4a-10=10

Constants are the numbers in equations that do not change. The variable in this equation is *a*. Variables are most commonly presented as either *x* or *y*, but they can be any letter. Every variable is equal to a number; one must solve the equation to determine what that number is. In an algebraic expression, the answer will usually be the number represented by the variable. In order to solve this equation, keep in mind that what is done to one side must be done to the other side as well. The first step will be to remove 10 from the left side by adding 10 to both sides. This will be expressed as 4a-10+10=10+10, which simplifies to 4a=20. Next, remove the 4 by dividing both sides by 4. This step will be expressed as 4a÷4=20÷4. The expression now becomes *a*=5.

Since variables are the letters that represent an unknown number, you must solve for that unknown number in single variable problems. The main thing to remember is that you can do anything to one side of an equation as long as you do it to the other.

EXAMPLE 2:

Solve for x in the equation 2x + 3 = 5.

Answer: First you want to get the "2x" isolated by itself on one side. To do that, first get rid of the 3. Subtract 3 from both sides of the equation 2x + 3 – 3 = 5 – 3 or 2x = 2. Now since the x is being multiplied by the 2 in "2x", you must divide by 2 to get rid of it. So, divide both sides by 2, which gives 2x / 2 = 2 / 2 or x = 1.

MANIPULATING EQUATIONS

Sometimes you will have variables missing in equations. So, you need to find the missing variable. To do this, you need to remember one important thing: whatever you do to one side of an equation, you need to do to the other side. If you subtract 100 from one side of an equation, you need to subtract 100 from the other side of the equation. This will allow you to change the form of the equation to find missing values.

EXAMPLE

Ray earns \$10 an hour. This can be given with the expression $10x$, where x is equal to the number of hours that Ray works. This is the independent variable. The independent variable is the amount that can change. The money that Ray earns is in y hours. So, you would write the equation: $10x = y$. The variable y is the dependent variable. This depends on x and cannot be changed. Now, let's say that Ray makes \$360. How many hours did he work to make \$360?

$$10x = 360$$

Now, you want to know how many hours that Ray worked. So, you want to get x by itself. To do that, you can divide both sides of the equation by 10.

$$\frac{10x}{10} = \frac{360}{10}$$

So, you have: $x = 36$. Now, you know that Ray worked 36 hours to make \$360.

POLYNOMIAL ALGEBRA

Equations are made up of monomials and polynomials. A *Monomial* is a single variable or product of constants and variables, such as x, $2x$, or $\frac{2}{x}$. There will never be addition or subtraction symbols in a

23

monomial. Like monomials have like variables, but they may have different coefficients. *Polynomials* are algebraic expressions which use addition and subtraction to combine two or more monomials. Two terms make a binomial; three terms make a trinomial; etc.. The *Degree of a Monomial* is the sum of the exponents of the variables. The *Degree of a Polynomial* is the highest degree of any individual term.

ADD POLYNOMIALS

To add polynomials, you need to add like terms. These terms have the same variable part. An example is $4x^2$ and $3x^2$ have x^2 terms. To find the sum of like terms, find the sum of the coefficients. Then, keep the same variable part. You can use the distributive property to distribute the plus sign to each term of the polynomial. For example:

$(4x^2 - 5x + 7) + (3x^2 + 2x + 1) =$

$(4x^2 - 5x + 7) + 3x^2 + 2x + 1 =$

$(4x^2 + 3x^2) + (-5x + 2x) + (7 + 1) =$

$$7x^2 - 3x + 8$$

SUBTRACT POLYNOMIALS

To subtract polynomials, you need to subtract like terms. To find the difference of like terms, find the difference of the coefficients. Then, keep the same variable part. You can use the distributive property to distribute the minus sign to each term of the polynomial. For example:

$(-2x^2 - x + 5) - (3x^2 - 4x + 1) =$

$(-2x^2 - x + 5) - 3x^2 + 4x - 1 =$

$(-2x^2 - 3x^2) + (-x + 4x) + (5 - 1) =$

$-5x^2 + 3x + 4$

MULTIPLY POLYNOMIALS

To multiply two binomials, follow the *FOIL* method. FOIL stands for:

- First: Multiply the first term of each binomial
- Outer: Multiply the outer terms of each binomial
- Inner: Multiply the inner terms of each binomial
- Last: Multiply the last term of each binomial

Using FOIL $(Ax + By)(Cx + Dy) = ACx^2 + ADxy + BCxy + BDy^2$.

Example: $(3x + 6)(4x - 2)$

First: $3x \times 4x = 12x^2$

Outer: $3x \times -2 = -6x$ | Current Expression: $12x^2 - 6x$

Inner: $6 \times 4x = 24x$ | Current Expression: $12x^2 - 6x + 24x$

Last: $6 \times -2 = -12$ | Final Expression: $12x^2 - 6x + 24x - 12$

Now, combine like terms. For this example, that is $-6x + 24x$. Then, the expression looks like: $12x^2 + 18x - 12$. Each number is a multiple of 6. So, the expression becomes $6(2x^2 + 3x - 2)$, and the polynomial has been expanded.

DIVIDE POLYNOMIALS

To divide polynomials, start with placing the terms of each polynomial in order of one variable. You may put them in ascending or descending order. Also, be consistent with both polynomials. To get the first term of the quotient, divide the first term of the dividend by the first term of the divisor. Next, multiply the first term of the quotient by the entire divisor. Then, subtract that product from the dividend and repeat for the following terms.

You want to end with a remainder of zero or a remainder with a degree that is less than the degree of the divisor. If the quotient has a remainder, write the answer as a mixed expression in the form: quotient $+ \frac{\text{remainder}}{\text{divisor}}$.

<u>Example 1:</u> Divide $4x^5 + 3x^2 - x$ by x

$$\frac{4x^5}{x} + \frac{3x^2}{x} - \frac{x}{x} = 4x^4 + 3x - 1$$

Example 2: Divide the polynomial $x^2 + 2x - 4$ by $(x - 3)$. Verify the Remainder Theorem by evaluating the polynomial at $x = 3$.

Divide the polynomial $x^2 + 2x - 4$ by $(x - 3)$ using synthetic or long division:

```
3| 1  2  -4              x  - 5
   |   3  15      x - 3 | x² + 2x - 4
   ---------            - x² + 3x
     1  5  11                 5x - 4
                              5x + 15
                                R 11
```

In either case, the remainder is 11. By the Remainder Theorem, for a polynomial $P(x)$ and a real number a, the remainder when $P(x)$ is divided by $(x - a)$ is $P(a)$. In this case, this means the remainder when $x^2 + 2x - 4$ is divided by $(x - 3)$ must be $P(3)$.

Verify that P(3) = 11 by substituting x = 3 into the polynomial: $(3)^2 + 2(3) - 4 = 9 + 6 - 4 = 11$

Below are patterns of some special products to remember: *perfect trinomial squares*, the *difference between two squares*, the *sum and difference of two cubes*, and *perfect cubes*.

- Perfect Trinomial Squares: $x^2 + 2xy + y^2 = (x + y)^2$ or $x^2 - 2xy + y^2 = (x - y)^2$
- Difference between Two Squares: $x^2 - y^2 = (x + y)(x - y)$
- Sum of Two Cubes: $x^3 + y^3 = (x + y)(x^2 - xy + y^2)$
  Note: the second factor is NOT the same as a perfect trinomial square. So, do not try to factor it further.
- Difference between Two Cubes: $x^3 - y^3 = (x - y)(x^2 + xy + y^2)$
  Again, the second factor is NOT the same as a perfect trinomial square.
- Perfect Cubes: $x^3 + 3x^2y + 3xy^2 + y^3 = (x + y)^3$ and $x^3 - 3x^2y + 3xy^2 - y^3 = (x - y)^3$

FACTOR A POLYNOMIAL

1. Check for a common monomial factor.
2. Factor out the greatest common monomial factor
3. Look for patterns of special products: differences of two squares, the sum or difference of two cubes for binomial factors, or perfect trinomial squares for trinomial factors.

EXAMPLE

Solve the equation $2x^2 - 5x - 12 = 0$ by factoring.

The expression $2x^2 - 5x - 12$ splits into two factors of the form $(2x + a)(x + b)$. To find a and b, you must find two factors of -12 that sum to -5 after one of them is doubled.

-12 can be factored in the following ways: 1 and -12 | 2 and -6 | 3 and -4 |

4 and -3 | 6 and -2 | 12 and -1.

Of these factors, only 3 and -4 will sum to -5 after we double one of them. Since -4 is the factor that must be doubled, it should go in position b, where it will be multiplied by $2x$ when the FOIL method is used. The factored expression is $(2x + 3)(x - 4)$. So, you are left with $(2x + 3)(x - 4) = 0$.

By the zero product property, each value of x that will make one of the factors equal zero is a solution to this equation. The first factor equals zero when $x = -1.5$, and the second factor equals zero when $x = 4$. So, those are the solutions.

Note: The factor may be a trinomial but not a perfect trinomial square. So, look for a factorable form: $x^2 + (a + b)x + ab = (x + a)(x + b)$

or $(ac)x^2 + (ad + bc)x + bd = (ax + b)(cx + d)$

Some factors may have four terms. So, look for groups to factor. After you have found the factors, write the original polynomial as the product of all the factors. Make sure that all of the polynomial factors are prime. Monomial factors may be prime or composite. Check your work by multiplying the factors to make sure you get the original polynomial.

Review Video: Polynomials
Visit mometrix.com/academy and enter code: 305005

SOLVING QUADRATIC EQUATIONS

The *Quadratic Formula* is used to solve quadratic equations when other methods are more difficult. To use the quadratic formula to solve a quadratic equation, begin by rewriting the equation in standard form $ax^2 + bx + c = 0$, where a, b, and c are coefficients. Once you have identified the values of the coefficients, substitute those values into the quadratic formula $= \frac{-b \pm \sqrt{b^2 - 4ac}}{2a}$. Evaluate the equation and simplify the expression. Again, check each root by substituting into the original equation. In the quadratic formula, the portion of the formula under the radical $(b^2 - 4ac)$ is called the *Discriminant*. If the discriminant is zero, there is only one root: zero. If the discriminant is positive, there are two different real roots. If the discriminant is negative, there are no real roots.

To solve a quadratic equation by *Factoring*, begin by rewriting the equation in standard form, if necessary. Factor the side with the variable then set each of the factors equal to zero and solve the resulting linear equations. Check your answers by substituting the roots you found into the original equation. If, when writing the equation in standard form, you have an equation in the form $x^2 + c =$

0 or $x^2 - c = 0$, set $x^2 = -c$ or $x^2 = c$ and take the square root of c. If $c = 0$, the only real root is zero. If c is positive, there are two real roots—the positive and negative square root values. If c is negative, there are no real roots because you cannot take the square root of a negative number.

To solve a quadratic equation by *Completing the Square*, rewrite the equation so that all terms containing the variable are on the left side of the equal sign, and all the constants are on the right side of the equal sign. Make sure the coefficient of the squared term is 1. If there is a coefficient with the squared term, divide each term on both sides of the equal side by that number. Next, work with the coefficient of the single-variable term. Square half of this coefficient, and add that value to both sides. Now you can factor the left side (the side containing the variable) as the square of a binomial. $x^2 + 2ax + a^2 = C \Rightarrow (x + a)^2 = C$, where x is the variable, and a and C are constants. Take the square root of both sides and solve for the variable. Substitute the value of the variable in the original problem to check your work.

In order to solve a *Radical Equation*, begin by isolating the radical term on one side of the equation, and move all other terms to the other side of the equation. Look at the index of the radicand. Remember, if no number is given, the index is 2, meaning square root. Raise both sides of the equation to the power equal to the index of the radical. Solve the resulting equation as you would a normal polynomial equation. When you have found the roots, you must check them in the original problem to eliminate extraneous roots.

> **Review Video: Using the Quadratic Formula**
> Visit mometrix.com/academy and enter code: 163102

INEQUALITIES

In algebra and higher areas of math, you will work with problems that do not equal each other. The statement comparing such expressions with symbols such as < (less than) or > (greater than) is called an *Inequality*.

One way to remember these symbols is to see that the sign for "less than" looks like an *L* for *Less*. *The terms less than or equal to, at most*, or *no more than* are for the symbol ≤. Also, the terms *greater than or equal to, at least*, and *no less than* are for the symbol ≥.

GRAPHING AND SOLVING INEQUALITIES

Solving inequalities can be done with the same rules as for solving equations. However, when multiplying or dividing by a negative number, the direction of the inequality sign must be flipped or reversed.

EXAMPLE 1

An example of an inequality is $7x > 5$. To solve for x, divide both sides by 7, and the solution is $x > \frac{5}{7}$. Graphs of the solution set of inequalities are given on a number line. Open circles are used to show that an expression approaches a number. However, the open circle points out that it is not equal to that number.

EXAMPLE 2

Graph $10 > -2x + 4$.

In order to graph the inequality $10 > -2x + 4$, you need to solve for x. The opposite of addition is subtraction. So, subtract 4 from both sides. This gives you $6 > -2x$.

Next, the opposite of multiplication is division. So, divide both sides by -2. Don't forget to flip the inequality symbol because you are dividing by a negative number. Now, you have $-3 < x$. You can rewrite this as $x > -3$.

To graph an inequality, you make a number line. Then, put a circle around the value that is being compared to x. If you are graphing a *greater than* or *less than* inequality, the circle remains open. This stands for all of the values except -3. If the inequality is *greater than or equal to* or *less than or equal to*, you draw a closed circle around the value. This would stand for all of the values including the number.

Finally, look over the values that the solution stands for. Then, shade the number line in the needed direction. This example calls for graphing all of the values greater than -3. This is all of the numbers to the right of -3. So, you shade this area on the number line.

OTHER INEQUALITIES

Conditional Inequalities are those with certain values for the variable that will make the condition true. So, other values for the variable where the condition will be false. *Absolute Inequalities* can have any real number as the value for the variable to make the condition true. So, there is no real number value for the variable that will make the condition false.

Double Inequalities are when two inequality statements are part of the same variable expression. An example of this is $-c < ax + b < c$.

IMPORTANT CONCEPTS

SUBSTITUTE AN INTEGER

POLYNOMIAL EXPRESSIONS

Solve the expression $(x^2+4)+(3x^2+4x+2)$, when x=5.

First, substitute in 5 for each occurrence of 'x': $(5^2 + 4) + (3(5)^2 + 4(5) + 2) =$

Second, solve for the parentheses: $(25 + 4) + (75 + 20 + 2) =$

Third, add the totals: $29 + 97 = 126$

LINEAR EXPRESSIONS

Solve the expression $(x - 4) + (4x + 10)$, when x=6.

First, put in 6 for every x: $(6 - 4) + (4(6) + 10)$

Second, solve the parentheses: $(2) + (34) =$

Third, add 2 and 34: $(2) + (34) = 36$

WRITING AN EXPRESSION FROM WORD-TO-SYMBOL

To write an expression, you must first put variables with the unknown values in the problem. Then, translate the words and phrases into expressions that have numbers and symbols.

INEQUALITIES

To write out an inequality, you may need to translate a sentence into an inequality. This translation is putting the words into symbols. When translating, choose a variable to stand for the unknown value. Then, change the words or phrases into symbols. For example, the sum of 2 and a number is at most 12. So, you would write: $2 + b \leq 12$.

Example: A farm sells vegetables and dairy products. One third of the sales from dairy products plus half of the sales from vegetables should be greater than the monthly payment (P) for the farm.

Let d stand for the sales from dairy products. Let v stand for the sales from vegetables. One third of the sales from dairy products is the expression $\frac{d}{3}$. One half of the sales from vegetables is the expression $\frac{v}{2}$. The sum of these expressions should be greater than the monthly payment for the farm. An inequality for this is $\frac{d}{3} + \frac{v}{2} > P$.

POLYNOMIAL EXPRESSIONS

Fred buys some CDs for $12 each. He also buys two DVDs. The total that Fred spent is $60. Write an equation that shows the connection between the number of CDs and the average cost of a DVD.

Let c stand for the number of CDs that Fred buys. Also, let d stand for the average cost of one of the DVDs that Fred buys. The expression $12c$ gives the cost of the CDs and the expression $2d$ gives the cost of the DVDs. So the equation $12c + 2d = 60$ states the number of CDs and the average cost of a DVD.

SOLVE EQUATIONS IN ONE VARIABLE

MANIPULATING EQUATIONS

Sometimes you will have variables missing in equations. So, you need to find the missing variable. To do this, you need to remember one important thing: whatever you do to one side of an equation, you need to do to the other side. If you subtract 100 from one side of an equation, you need to subtract 100 from the other side of the equation. This will allow you to change the form of the equation to find missing values.

EXAMPLE

Ray earns $10 an hour. This can be given with the expression $10x$, where x is equal to the number of hours that Ray works. This is the independent variable. The independent variable is the amount that can change. The money that Ray earns is in y hours. So, you would write the equation: $10x = y$. The variable y is the dependent variable. This depends on x and cannot be changed. Now, let's say that Ray makes $360. How many hours did he work to make $360?

$$10x = 360$$

Now, you want to know how many hours that Ray worked. So, you want to get x by itself. To do that, you can divide both sides of the equation by 10.

$$\frac{10x}{10} = \frac{360}{10}$$

So, you have: $x = 36$. Now, you know that Ray worked 36 hours to make $360.

SOLVING ONE VARIABLE LINEAR EQUATIONS

Another way to write an equation is $ax + b = 0$ where $a \neq 0$. This is known as a *One Variable Linear Equation*. A solution to an equation is called a *Root*.

Example: $5x + 10 = 0$

If we solve for x, the solution is $x = -2$. In other words, the root of the equation is -2.

The first step is to subtract 10 from both sides. This gives $5x = -10$.

Next, divide both sides by the coefficient of the variable. For this example, that is 5. So, you should have $x = -2$. You can make sure that you have the correct answer by placing -2 back into the original equation. So, the equation now looks like this: $(5)(-2) + 10 = -10 + 10 = 0$.

The *Solution Set* is the set of all solutions to an equation. In the last example, the solution set would be -2. If there were more solutions, then they would also be included in the solution set. Usually, there are more solutions in multivariable equations. When an equation has no true solutions, this is known as an *Empty Set*. Equations with identical solution sets are *Equivalent Equations*. An *Identity* is a term whose value or determinant is equal to 1.

To solve a *Radical Equation*, start by placing the radical term on one side of the equation by itself. Then, move all other terms to the other side of the equation. Look at the index of the radical symbol. Remember, if no number is given, then you have a square root. Raise both sides of the equation to the power equal to the index of the radical. Solve the equation as you would a normal polynomial equation. When you have found the roots, you must check them in the original problem to remove any remaining roots.

SYSTEMS OF EQUATIONS

Systems of Equations are a set of simultaneous equations that all use the same variables. A solution to a system of equations must be true for each equation in the system. *Consistent Systems* are those with at least one solution. *Inconsistent Systems* are systems of equations that have no solution. The two most common ways are *substitution* and *elimination*.

> **Review Video: <u>Systems of Equations</u>**
> Visit mometrix.com/academy and enter code: 658153

To solve a system of linear equations by *substitution*, start with the easier equation and solve for one of the variables. Express this variable in terms of the other variable. Substitute this expression in the other equation, and solve for the other variable. The solution should be expressed in the form (x, y). Substitute the values into both of the original equations to check your answer. Consider the following problem.

Solve the system using substitution:

$$x + 6y = 15$$

$$3x - 12y = 18$$

$$x = 15 - 6y$$

$$3(15 - 6y) - 12y = 18$$

$$45 - 18y - 12y = 18$$

$$30y = 27$$

$$y = \frac{27}{30} = \frac{9}{10} = 0.9$$

$$x = 15 - 6(0.9) = 15 - 5.4 = 9.6$$

Now check both equations

$$9.6 + 6(0.9) = 9.6 + 5.4 = 15$$

$$3(9.6) - 12(0.9) = 28.8 - 10.8 = 18$$

Therefore, the solution is (9.6, 0.9).

To solve a system of equations using *elimination* or *addition*, begin by rewriting both equations in standard form $Ax + By = C$. Check to see if the coefficients of one pair of like variables add to zero. If not, multiply one or both of the equations by a non-zero number to make one set of like variables add to zero. Add the two equations to solve for one of the variables. Substitute this value into one of the original equations to solve for the other variable. Check your work by substituting into the other equation. Next we will solve the same problem as above, but using the addition method.

Solve the system using substitution:

$$x + 6y = 15$$

$$3x - 12y = 18$$

For practice we will multiply the first equation by 6 and the second equation by -2 to get rid of the x variables.

$$6x + 36y = 90$$

$$-6x + 24y = -36$$

Add the equations together to get $60y = 54$. Thus, $y = \frac{54}{60} = \frac{9}{10} = 0.9$.

Plug the value for y back in to either of the original equations to get the value for x.

$$x + 6(0.9) = 15$$

$$x = 15 - 5.4 = 9.6$$

Now check both equations

$$9.6 + 6(0.9) = 9.6 + 5.4 = 15$$

$$3(9.6) - 12(0.9) = 28.8 - 10.8 = 18$$

Therefore, the solution is (9.6, 0.9).

Geometry

LINES AND PLANES

A point is a fixed location in space; has no size or dimensions; commonly represented by a dot.

A line is a set of points that extends infinitely in two opposite directions. It has length, but no width or depth. A line can be defined by any two distinct points that it contains. A line segment is a portion of a line that has definite endpoints. A ray is a portion of a line that extends from a single point on that line in one direction along the line. It has a definite beginning, but no ending.

A **plane** is a two-dimensional flat surface defined by three non-collinear points. A plane extends an infinite distance in all directions in those two dimensions. It contains an infinite number of points, parallel lines and segments, intersecting lines and segments, as well as parallel or intersecting rays. A plane will never contain a three-dimensional figure or skew lines, which are lines that don't intersect and are not parallel. Two given planes are either parallel or they intersect at a line. A plane may intersect a circular conic surface to form **conic sections**, such as a parabola, hyperbola, circle or ellipse.

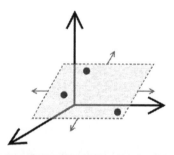

Review Video: Lines and Planes
Visit mometrix.com/academy and enter code: 554267

Perpendicular lines are lines that intersect at right angles. They are represented by the symbol ⊥. The shortest distance from a line to a point not on the line is a perpendicular segment from the point to the line.

Parallel lines are lines in the same plane that have no points in common and never meet. It is possible for lines to be in different planes, have no points in common, and never meet, but they are not parallel because they are in different planes.

A bisector is a line or line segment that divides another line segment into two equal lengths. A perpendicular bisector of a line segment is composed of points that are equidistant from the endpoints of the segment it is dividing.

Intersecting lines are lines that have exactly one point in common. Concurrent lines are multiple lines that intersect at a single point.

A transversal is a line that intersects at least two other lines, which may or may not be parallel to one another. A transversal that intersects parallel lines is a common occurrence in geometry.

COORDINATE PLANE

When algebraic functions and equations are shown graphically, they are usually shown on a *Cartesian Coordinate Plane*. The Cartesian coordinate plane consists of two number lines placed perpendicular to each other, and intersecting at the zero point, also known as the origin. The horizontal number line is known as the x-axis, with positive values to the right of the origin, and negative values to the left of the origin. The vertical number line is known as the y-axis, with positive values above the origin, and negative values below the origin.

Any point on the plane can be identified by an ordered pair in the form (x,y), called coordinates. The x-value of the coordinate is called the abscissa, and the y-value of the coordinate is called the ordinate. The two number lines divide the plane into four quadrants: I, II, III, and IV.

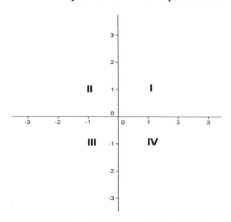

Before learning the different forms equations can be written in, it is important to understand some terminology. A ratio of the change in the vertical distance to the change in horizontal distance is called the *Slope*. On a graph with two points, (x_1, y_1) and (x_2, y_2), the slope is represented by the formula $= \frac{y_2 - y_1}{x_2 - x_1}$; $x_1 \neq x_2$. If the value of the slope is positive, the line slopes upward from left to right. If the value of the slope is negative, the line slopes downward from left to right. If the y-coordinates are the same for both points, the slope is 0 and the line is a *Horizontal Line*. If the x-coordinates are the same for both points, there is no slope and the line is a *Vertical Line*. Two or more lines that have equal slopes are *Parallel Lines*. *Perpendicular Lines* have slopes that are negative reciprocals of each other, such as $\frac{a}{b}$ and $\frac{-b}{a}$.

As mentioned previously, equations can be written many ways. Below is a list of the many forms equations can take.

- Standard Form: $Ax + By = C$; the slope is $\frac{-A}{B}$ and the y-intercept is $\frac{C}{B}$
- *Slope Intercept Form*: $y = mx + b$, where m is the slope and b is the y-intercept
- Point-Slope Form: $y - y_1 = m(x - x_1)$, where m is the slope and (x_1, y_1) is a point on the line
- Two-Point Form: $\frac{y - y_1}{x - x_1} = \frac{y_2 - y_1}{x_2 - x_1}$, where (x_1, y_1) and (x_2, y_2) are two points on the given line
- *Intercept Form*: $\frac{x}{x_1} + \frac{y}{y_1} = 1$, where $(x_1, 0)$ is the point at which a line intersects the x-axis, and $(0, y_1)$ is the point at which the same line intersects the y-axis

CALCULATIONS USING POINTS

Sometimes you need to perform calculations using only points on a graph as input data. Using points, you can determine what the midpoint and distance are. If you know the equation for a line you can calculate the distance between the line and the point.

To find the *Midpoint* of two points (x_1, y_1) and (x_2, y_2), average the x-coordinates to get the x-coordinate of the midpoint, and average the y-coordinates to get the y-coordinate of the midpoint. The formula is midpoint $= \left(\frac{x_1 + x_2}{2}, \frac{y_1 + y_2}{2} \right)$.

The *Distance* between two points is the same as the length of the hypotenuse of a right triangle with the two given points as endpoints, and the two sides of the right triangle parallel to the x-axis and y-axis, respectively. The length of the segment parallel to the x-axis is the difference between the x-coordinates of the two points. The length of the segment parallel to the y-axis is the difference between the y-coordinates of the two points. Use the Pythagorean Theorem $a^2 + b^2 = c^2$ or $c = \sqrt{a^2 + b^2}$ to find the distance. The formula is: distance $= \sqrt{(x_2 - x_1)^2 + (y_2 - y_1)^2}$.

When a line is in the format $Ax + By + C = 0$, where A, B, and C are coefficients, you can use a point (x_1, y_1) not on the line and apply the formula $d = \frac{|Ax_1 + By_1 + C|}{\sqrt{A^2 + B^2}}$ to find the distance between the line and the point (x_1, y_1).

> **Review Video: <u>Distance & Midpoint for Points on the Coordinate Plane</u>**
> Visit mometrix.com/academy and enter code: 973653

TRANSFORMATION

- Rotation: An object is rotated, or turned, between 0 and 360 degrees, around a fixed point. The size and shape of the object are unchanged.
- Reflection: An object is reflected, or flipped, across a line, so that the original object and reflected object are the same distance from the line of reflection. The size and shape of the object are unchanged.
- Translation: An object is translated, or shifted, horizontally and/or vertically to a new location. The orientation, size, and shape of the object are unchanged.

ROTATION

A line segment begins at (1, 4) and ends at (5, 4). Draw the line segment and rotate the line segment 90º about the point (3, 4).

The point about which the line segment is being rotated is on the line segment. This point should be on both the original and rotated line. The point (3, 4) is the center of the original line segment, and should still be the center of the rotated line segment. The dashed line is the rotated line segment.

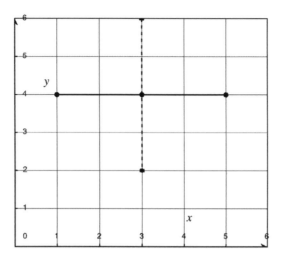

REFLECTION

Example 1: To create a congruent rectangle by reflecting, first draw a line of reflection. The line can be next to or on the figure. Then draw the image reflected across this line.

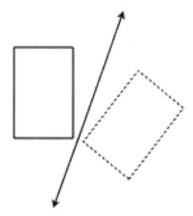

Example 2: A line segment begins at (1, 5) and ends at (5, 4). Draw the line segment, then reflect the line segment across the line $y = 3$.

To reflect a segment, consider folding a piece of paper at the line of reflection. The new image should line up exactly with the old image when the paper is folded. The dashed line is the reflected line segment.

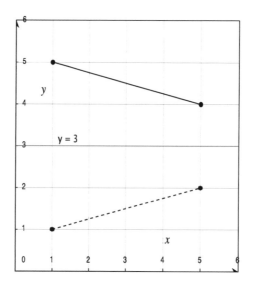

TRANSLATION

Example 1: A line segment on an x-y grid starts at (3, 2) and ends at (4, 1). Draw the line segment, and translate the segment up 2 units and left 2 units.

The solid line segment is the original line segment, and the dashed line is the translated line segment. The y-coordinate of each point has increased by 2, because the points moved two units away from 0. The x-coordinate of each point has decreased by 2, because the points moved two units closer to 0.

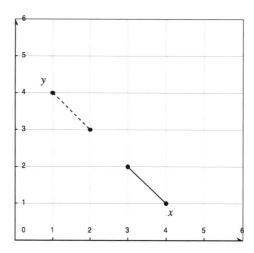

Example 2: Identify a transformation that could have been performed on the solid triangle to result in the dashed triangle.

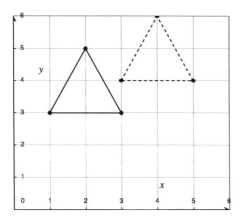

The transformed triangle has the same orientation as the original triangle. It has been shifted up one unit and two units to the right. Because the orientation of the figure has not changed, and its new position can be described using shifts up and to the right, the figure was translated.

Reading

Key Ideas and Details

SUMMARIZING A COMPLEX TEXT
SUMMARIZE

A helpful tool is the ability to summarize the information that you have read in a paragraph or passage format. This process is similar to creating an effective outline. First, a summary should accurately define the main idea of the passage though the summary does not need to explain this main idea in exhaustive detail. The summary should continue by laying out the most important supporting details or arguments from the passage. All of the significant supporting details should be included, and none of the details included should be irrelevant or insignificant. Also, the summary should accurately report all of these details. Too often, the desire for brevity in a summary leads to the sacrifice of clarity or accuracy. Summaries are often difficult to read because they omit all of the graceful language, digressions, and asides that distinguish great writing. However, an effective summary should contain much the same message as the original text.

PARAPHRASE

Paraphrasing is another method that the reader can use to aid in comprehension. When paraphrasing, one puts what they have read into their words by rephrasing what the author has written, or one "translates" all of what the author shared into their words by including as many details as they can.

TOPICS, MAIN IDEAS, AND SUPPORTING DETAILS
TOPICS AND MAIN IDEAS

One of the most important skills in reading comprehension is the identification of **topics** and **main ideas.** There is a subtle difference between these two features. The topic is the **subject** of a text (i.e., what the text is all about). The main idea, on the other hand, is the **most important point** being made by the author. The topic is usually expressed in a few words at the most while the main idea often needs a full sentence to be completely defined. As an example, a short passage might have the topic of penguins and the main idea could be written as *Penguins are different from other birds in many ways.* In most nonfiction writing, the topic and the main idea will be stated directly and often appear in a sentence at the very beginning or end of the text. When being tested on an understanding of the author's topic, you may be able to skim the passage for the general idea, by reading only the first sentence of each paragraph. A body paragraph's first sentence is often—but not always—the main topic sentence which gives you a summary of the content in the paragraph.

However, there are cases in which the reader must figure out an unstated topic or main idea. In these instances, you must read every sentence of the text and try to come up with an overarching idea that is supported by each of those sentences.

> **Review Video: Topics and Main Ideas**
> Visit mometrix.com/academy and enter code: 407801

SUPPORTING DETAILS

Supporting details provide evidence and backing for the main point. In order to show that a main idea is correct, or valid, authors add details that prove their point. All texts contain details, but they are only classified as supporting details when they serve to reinforce some larger point. Supporting

38

details are most commonly found in informative and persuasive texts. In some cases, they will be clearly indicated with terms like *for example* or *for instance*, or they will be enumerated with terms like *first*, *second*, and *last*. However, you need to be prepared for texts that do not contain those indicators. As a reader, you should consider whether the author's supporting details really back up his or her main point. Supporting details can be factual and correct, yet they may not be relevant to the author's point. Conversely, supporting details can seem pertinent, but they can be ineffective because they are based on opinion or assertions that cannot be proven.

> **Review Video: <u>Supporting Details</u>**
> Visit mometrix.com/academy and enter code: 396297

TOPIC AND SUMMARY SENTENCES

Topic and summary sentences are a convenient way to encapsulate the main idea of a text. In some textbooks and academic articles, the author will place a topic or summary sentence at the beginning of each section as a means of preparing the reader for what is to come. Research suggests that the brain is more receptive to new information when it has been prepared by the presentation of the main idea or some key words. The phenomenon is somewhat akin to the primer coat of paint that allows subsequent coats of paint to absorb more easily. A good topic sentence will be clear and not contain any jargon. When topic or summary sentences are not provided, good readers can jot down their own so that they can find their place in a text and refresh their memory.

IDENTIFYING THE LOGICAL CONCLUSION

Identifying a logical conclusion can help you determine whether you agree with the writer or not. Coming to this conclusion is much like making an inference: the approach requires you to combine the information given by the text with what you already know in order to make a logical conclusion. If the author intended the reader to draw a certain conclusion, then you can expect the author's argumentation and detail to be leading in that direction. One way to approach the task of drawing conclusions is to make brief notes of all the points made by the author. When the notes are arranged on paper, they may clarify the logical conclusion. Another way to approach conclusions is to consider whether the reasoning of the author raises any pertinent questions. Sometimes you will be able to draw several conclusions from a passage. On occasion these will be conclusions that were never imagined by the author. Therefore, be aware that these conclusions must be supported directly by the text.

DIRECTLY STATED INFORMATION

A reader should always be drawing conclusions from the text. Sometimes conclusions are implied from written information, and other times the information is **stated directly** within the passage. One should always aim to draw conclusions from information stated within a passage, rather than to draw them from mere implications. At times an author may provide some information and then describe a counterargument. Readers should be alert for direct statements that are subsequently rejected or weakened by the author. Furthermore, you should always read through the entire passage before drawing conclusions. Many readers are trained to expect the author's conclusions at either the beginning or the end of the passage, but many texts do not adhere to this format.

INFERENCES

Readers are often required to understand a text that claims and suggests ideas without stating them directly. An **inference** is a piece of information that is implied but not written outright by the author. For instance, consider the following sentence: *After the final out of the inning, the fans were filled with joy and rushed the field.* From this sentence, a reader can infer that the fans were watching a baseball game and their team won the game. Readers should take great care to avoid

39

using information beyond the provided passage before making inferences. As you practice drawing inferences, you will find that they require concentration and attention.

Test-taking tip: While being tested on your ability to make correct inferences, you must look for contextual clues. An answer can be *true* but not *correct*. The contextual clues will help you find the answer that is the best answer out of the given choices. Be careful in your reading to understand the context in which a phrase is stated. When asked for the implied meaning of a statement made in the passage, you should immediately locate the statement and read the context in which the statement was made. Also, look for an answer choice that has a similar phrase to the statement in question.

IMPLICATIONS

Drawing conclusions from information implied within a passage requires confidence on the part of the reader. **Implications** are things that the author does not state directly, but readers can assume based on what the author does say. Consider the following passage: *I stepped outside and opened my umbrella. By the time I got to work, the cuffs of my pants were soaked*. The author never states that it is raining, but this fact is clearly implied. Conclusions based on implication must be well supported by the text. In order to draw a solid conclusion, readers should have multiple pieces of evidence. If readers have only one piece, they must be assured that there is no other possible explanation than their conclusion. A good reader will be able to draw many conclusions from information implied by the text which will be a great help in the exam.

THEMES IN PRINT AND OTHER SOURCES

Themes are seldom expressed directly in a text and can be difficult to identify. A theme is an issue, an idea, or a question raised by the text. For instance, a theme of *Cinderella* (the Charles Perrault version) is perseverance as the title character serves her step-sisters and step-mother, and the prince seeks to find the girl with the missing slipper. A passage may have many themes, and you, as a dedicated reader, must take care to identify only themes that you are asked to find. One common characteristic of themes is that they raise more questions than they answer. In a good piece of fiction, authors are trying to elevate the reader's perspective and encourage him or her to consider the themes in a deeper way. In the process of reading, one can identify themes by constantly asking about the general issues that the text is addressing. A good way to evaluate an author's approach to a theme is to begin reading with a question in mind (e.g., How does this text approach the theme of love?) and to look for evidence in the text that addresses that question.

SIMILAR THEMES ACROSS CULTURES

A brief study of world literature suggests that writers from vastly different cultures address similar themes. For instance, works like the *Odyssey* and *Hamlet* both consider the individual's battle for self-control and independence. In most cultures, authors address themes of personal growth and the struggle for maturity. Another universal theme is the conflict between the individual and society. Works that are as culturally disparate as *Native Son*, the *Aeneid*, and *1984* dramatize how people struggle to maintain their personalities and dignity in large (sometimes) oppressive groups. Finally, many cultures have versions of the hero's or heroine's journey in which an adventurous person must overcome many obstacles in order to gain greater knowledge, power, and perspective.

Some famous works that treat this theme are the *Epic of Gilgamesh*, Dante's *Divine Comedy*, and Cervantes' *Don Quixote.*

DIFFERENCES IN ADDRESSING THEMES IN VARIOUS CULTURES AND GENRES

Authors from different genres and cultures may address similar themes, but they do so in different ways. For instance, poets are likely to address subject matter indirectly through the use of images and allusions. In a play, the author is more likely to dramatize themes by using characters to express opposing viewpoints; this disparity is known as a dialectical approach. In a passage, the author does not need to express themes directly; indeed, they can be expressed through events and actions. In some regional literatures, such as Greece or England, authors use more irony: their works have characters that express views and make decisions that are clearly disapproved of by the author. In Latin America, there is a great tradition of using supernatural events to illustrate themes about real life. Chinese and Japanese authors frequently use well-established regional forms (e.g., haiku poetry in Japan) to organize their treatment of universal themes.

Organization and Purpose

ORGANIZATION OF THE TEXT

The way a text is organized can help readers to understand the author's intent and his or her conclusions. There are various ways to organize a text, and each one has a purpose and use.

Some nonfiction texts are organized to **present a problem** followed by a solution. For this type of text, the problem is often explained before the solution is offered. In some cases, as when the problem is well known, the solution may be introduced briefly at the beginning. Other passages may focus on the solution, and the problem will be referenced only occasionally. Some texts will outline multiple solutions to a problem, leaving readers to choose among them. If the author has an interest or an allegiance to one solution, he or she may fail to mention or describe accurately some of the other solutions. Readers should be careful of the author's agenda when reading a problem-solution text. Only by understanding the author's perspective and interests can one develop a proper judgment of the proposed solution.

Occasionally, authors will organize information logically in a passage so the reader can follow and locate the information within the text. Since this is not always the case with passages in an exam, you need to be familiar with other examples of provided information. Two common organizational structures are cause and effect and chronological order. When using **chronological order**, the author presents information in the order that it happened. For example, biographies are written in chronological order. The subject's birth and childhood are presented first, followed by their adult life, and lastly by the events leading up to the person's death.

In **cause and effect**, an author presents one thing that makes something else happen. For example, if one were to go to bed very late and awake very early, then they would be tired in the morning. The cause is lack of sleep, with the effect of being tired the next day.

Identifying the cause-and-effect relationships in a text can be tricky, but there are a few ways to approach this task. Often, these relationships are signaled with certain terms. When an author uses words like *because*, *since*, *in order*, and *so*, he or she is likely describing a cause-and-effect relationship. Consider the sentence: *He called her because he needed the homework*. This is a simple causal relationship in which the cause was his need for the homework, and the effect was his phone call. Yet, not all cause-and-effect relationships are marked in this way. Consider the sentences: *He called her. He needed the homework*. When the cause-and-effect relationship is not indicated with a keyword, the relationship can be discovered by asking why something happened. He called her: why? The answer is in the next sentence: He needed the homework.

Persuasive essays, in which an author tries to make a convincing argument and change the minds of readers, usually include cause-and-effect relationships. However, these relationships should not always be taken at face value. Frequently, an author will assume a cause or take an effect for granted. To read a persuasive essay effectively, readers need to judge the cause-and-effect relationships that the author is presenting. For instance, imagine an author wrote the following: *The parking deck has been unprofitable because people would prefer to ride their bikes.* The relationship is clear: the cause is that people prefer to ride their bikes, and the effect is that the parking deck has been unprofitable. However, readers should consider whether this argument is conclusive. Perhaps there are other reasons for the failure of the parking deck: a down economy, excessive fees, etc. Too often, authors present causal relationships as if they are fact rather than opinion. Readers should be on the alert for these dubious claims.

Many texts follow the **compare-and-contrast** model in which the similarities and differences between two ideas or things are explored. Analysis of the similarities between ideas is called comparison. In an ideal comparison, the author places ideas or things in an equivalent structure (i.e., the author presents the ideas in the same way). If an author wants to show the similarities between cricket and baseball, then he or she may do so by summarizing the equipment and rules for each game. Be mindful of the similarities as they appear in the passage and take note of any differences that are mentioned. Often, these small differences will only reinforce the more general similarity.

Thinking critically about ideas and conclusions can seem like a daunting task. One way to ease this task is to understand the basic elements of ideas and writing techniques. Looking at the way different ideas relate to each other can be a good way for readers to begin their analysis. For instance, sometimes authors will write about two ideas that are in opposition to each other. Or one author will provide his or her ideas on a topic, and another author may respond in opposition. The analysis of these opposing ideas is known as **contrast**. Contrast is often marred by the author's obvious partiality to one of the ideas. A discerning reader will be put off by an author who does not engage in a fair fight. In an analysis of opposing ideas, both ideas should be presented in clear and reasonable terms. If the author does prefer a side, you need to read carefully to determine the areas where the author shows or avoids this preference. In an analysis of opposing ideas, you should proceed through the passage by marking the major differences point by point with an eye that is looking for an explanation of each side's view. For instance, in an analysis of capitalism and communism, there is an importance in outlining each side's view on labor, markets, prices, personal responsibility, etc. Additionally, as you read through the passages, you should note whether the opposing views present each side in a similar manner.

PURPOSES FOR WRITING

In order to be an effective reader, one must pay attention to the author's **position** and purpose. Even those texts that seem objective and impartial, like textbooks, have a position and bias. Readers need to take these positions into account when considering the author's message. When an author uses emotional language or clearly favors one side of an argument, his or her position is clear. However, the author's position may be evident not only in what he or she writes, but also in what he or she doesn't write. In a normal setting, a reader would want to review some other texts on the same topic in order to develop a view of the author's position. If this was not possible, then you would want to acquire some background about the author. However, since you are in the middle of an exam and the only source of information is the text, you should look for language and argumentation that seems to indicate a particular stance on the subject.

> **Review Video: Author's Position**
> Visit mometrix.com/academy and enter code: 827954

Usually, identifying the **purpose** of an author is easier than identifying his or her position. In most cases, the author has no interest in hiding his or her purpose. A text that is meant to entertain, for instance, should be written to please the reader. Most narratives, or stories, are written to entertain, though they may also inform or persuade. Informative texts are easy to identify, while the most difficult purpose of a text to identify is persuasion because the author has an interest in making this purpose hard to detect. When a reader discovers that the author is trying to persuade, he or she should be skeptical of the argument. For this reason persuasive texts often try to establish an entertaining tone and hope to amuse the reader into agreement. On the other hand, an informative tone may be implemented to create an appearance of authority and objectivity.

An author's purpose is evident often in the organization of the text (e.g., section headings in bold font points to an informative text). However, you may not have such organization available to you in your exam. Instead, if the author makes his or her main idea clear from the beginning, then the likely purpose of the text is to inform. If the author begins by making a claim and provides various arguments to support that claim, then the purpose is probably to persuade. If the author tells a story or seems to want the attention of the reader more than to push a particular point or deliver information, then his or her purpose is most likely to entertain. As a reader, you must judge authors on how well they accomplish their purpose. In other words, you need to consider the type of passage (e.g., technical, persuasive, etc.) that the author has written and whether the author has followed the requirements of the passage type.

> **Review Video: <u>Purpose of an Author</u>**
> Visit mometrix.com/academy and enter code: 497555

The author's purpose for writing will affect his or her writing style and the response of the reader. In a **persuasive essay**, the author is attempting to change the reader's mind or convince him or her of something that he or she did not believe previously. There are several identifying characteristics of persuasive writing. One is opinion presented as fact. When authors attempt to persuade readers, they often present their opinions as if they were fact. Readers must be on guard for statements that sound factual but which cannot be subjected to research, observation, or experiment. Another characteristic of persuasive writing is emotional language. An author will often try to play on the emotions of readers by appealing to their sympathy or sense of morality. When an author uses colorful or evocative language with the intent of arousing the reader's passions, then the author may be attempting to persuade. Finally, in many cases, a persuasive text will give an unfair explanation of opposing positions, if these positions are mentioned at all.

An **informative text** is written to educate and enlighten readers. Informative texts are almost always nonfiction and are rarely structured as a story. The intention of an informative text is to deliver information in the most comprehensible way. So, look for the structure of the text to be very clear. In an informative text, the thesis statement is one or two sentences that normally appears at the end of the first paragraph. The author may use some colorful language, but he or she is likely to put more emphasis on clarity and precision. Informative essays do not typically appeal to the emotions. They often contain facts and figures and rarely include the opinion of the author; however, readers should remain aware of the possibility for a bias as those facts are presented. Sometimes a persuasive essay can resemble an informative essay, especially if the author maintains an even tone and presents his or her views as if they were established fact.

The success or failure of an author's intent to **entertain** is determined by those who read the author's work. Entertaining texts may be either fiction or nonfiction, and they may describe real or imagined people, places, and events. Entertaining texts are often narratives or poems. A text that is written to entertain is likely to contain colorful language that engages the imagination and the emotions. Such writing often features a great deal of figurative language, which typically enlivens the subject matter with images and analogies.

Though an entertaining text is not usually written to persuade or inform, authors may accomplish both of these tasks in their work. An entertaining text may appeal to the reader's emotions and cause him or her to think differently about a particular subject. In any case, entertaining texts tend to showcase the personality of the author more than other types of writing.

When an author intends to **express feelings,** he or she may use expressive and bold language. An author may write with emotion for any number of reasons. Sometimes, authors will express feelings because they are describing a personal situation of great pain or happiness. In other situations, authors will attempt to persuade the reader and will use emotion to stir up the passions. This kind of expression is easy to identify when the writer uses phrases like *I felt* and *I sense*. However, readers may find that the author will simply describe feelings without introducing them. As a reader, you must know the importance of recognizing when an author is expressing emotion and not to become overwhelmed by sympathy or passion. Readers should maintain some detachment so that they can still evaluate the strength of the author's argument or the quality of the writing.

In a sense, almost all writing is descriptive, insofar as an author seeks to describe events, ideas, or people to the reader. Some texts, however, are primarily concerned with **description**. A descriptive text focuses on a particular subject and attempts to depict the subject in a way that will be clear to readers. Descriptive texts contain many adjectives and adverbs (i.e., words that give shades of meaning and create a more detailed mental picture for the reader). A descriptive text fails when it is unclear to the reader. A descriptive text will certainly be informative and may be persuasive and entertaining as well.

Building a Vocabulary

The **denotative** meaning of a word is the literal meaning. The **connotative** meaning goes beyond the denotative meaning to include the emotional reaction that a word may invoke. The connotative meaning often takes the denotative meaning a step further due to associations which the reader makes with the denotative meaning. Readers can differentiate between the denotative and connotative meanings by first recognizing how authors use each meaning. Most nonfiction, for example, is fact-based, and nonfiction authors rarely use flowery, figurative language. The reader can assume that the writer is using the denotative meaning of words. In fiction, the author may use the connotative meaning. Readers can determine whether the author is using the denotative or connotative meaning of a word by implementing context clues.

Review Video: Denotation and Connotation
Visit mometrix.com/academy and enter code: 310092

Readers of all levels will encounter words that they either have never seen or have only encountered on a limited basis. The best way to define a word in **context** is to look for nearby words that can assist in learning the meaning of the word. For instance, unfamiliar nouns are often accompanied by examples that provide a definition. Consider the following sentence: *Dave arrived at the party in hilarious garb: a leopard-print shirt, buckskin trousers, and high heels.* If a reader was unfamiliar with the meaning of garb, he or she could read the examples (i.e., a leopard-print shirt, buckskin trousers, and high heels) and quickly determine that the word means *clothing*. Examples will not always be this obvious. Consider this sentence: *Parsley, lemon, and flowers were just a few of items he used as garnishes.* Here, the word *garnishes* is exemplified by parsley, lemon, and flowers. Readers who have eaten in a few restaurants will probably be able to identify a garnish as something used to decorate a plate.

Review Video: Context
Visit mometrix.com/academy and enter code: 613660

In addition to looking at the context of a passage, readers can use contrasts to define an unfamiliar word in context. In many sentences, the author will not describe the unfamiliar word directly; instead, he or she will describe the opposite of the unfamiliar word. Thus, you are provided with some information that will bring you closer to defining the word. Consider the following example: *Despite his intelligence, Hector's low brow and bad posture made him look obtuse.* The author writes that Hector's appearance does not convey intelligence. Therefore, *obtuse* must mean unintelligent. Here is another example: *Despite the horrible weather, we were beatific about our trip to Alaska.* The word *despite* indicates that the speaker's feelings were at odds with the weather. Since the weather is described as *horrible*, then *beatific* must mean something positive.

In some cases, there will be very few contextual clues to help a reader define the meaning of an unfamiliar word. When this happens, one strategy that readers may employ is **substitution**. A good reader will brainstorm some possible synonyms for the given word, and he or she will substitute these words into the sentence. If the sentence and the surrounding passage continue to make sense, then the substitution has revealed at least some information about the unfamiliar word. Consider the sentence: *Frank's admonition rang in her ears as she climbed the mountain.* A reader unfamiliar with *admonition* might come up with some substitutions like *vow, promise, advice, complaint,* or *compliment.* All of these words make general sense of the sentence though their meanings are diverse. The process has suggested; however, that an admonition is some sort of message. The substitution strategy is rarely able to pinpoint a precise definition, but this process can be effective as a last resort.

46

Occasionally, you will be able to define an unfamiliar word by looking at the descriptive words in the context. Consider the following sentence: *Fred dragged the recalcitrant boy kicking and screaming up the stairs.* The words *dragged*, *kicking*, and *screaming* all suggest that the boy does not want to go up the stairs. The reader may assume that *recalcitrant* means something like unwilling or protesting. In this example, an unfamiliar adjective was identified.

Additionally, using description to define an unfamiliar noun is a common practice compared to unfamiliar adjectives, as in this sentence: *Don's wrinkled frown and constantly shaking fist identified him as a curmudgeon of the first order.* Don is described as having a *wrinkled frown and constantly shaking fist* suggesting that a *curmudgeon* must be a grumpy person. Contrasts do not always provide detailed information about the unfamiliar word, but they at least give the reader some clues.

When a word has more than one meaning, readers can have difficulty with determining how the word is being used in a given sentence. For instance, the verb *cleave*, can mean either *join* or *separate*. When readers come upon this word, they will have to select the definition that makes the most sense. Consider the following sentence: *Hermione's knife cleaved the bread cleanly.* Since, a knife cannot join bread together, the word must indicate separation. A slightly more difficult example would be the sentence: *The birds cleaved together as they flew from the oak tree.* Immediately, the presence of the word *together* should suggest that in this sentence *cleave* is being used to mean *join*. Discovering the intent of a word with multiple meanings requires the same tricks as defining an unknown word: look for contextual clues and evaluate the substituted words.

As a person is exposed to more words, the extent of their vocabulary will expand. By reading on a regular basis, a person can increase the number of ways that they have seen a word in context. Based on experience, a person can recall how a word was used in the past and apply that knowledge to a new context. For example, a person may have seen the word *gull* used to mean a bird that is found near the seashore. However, a *gull* can be a person who is tricked easily. If the word in context is used in reference to a character, the reader can recognize the insult since gulls are not seen as extremely intelligent. When you use your knowledge about a word, you can find comparisons or figure out the meaning for a new use of a word.

Word Meaning from Context

One of the benefits of reading is the expansion of one's vocabulary. In order to obtain this benefit, however, one needs to know how to identify the definition of a word from its context. This means defining a word based on the words around it and the way it is used in a sentence. Consider the following sentence: *The elderly scholar spent his evenings hunched over arcane texts that few other people even knew existed.* The adjective *arcane* is uncommon, but you can obtain significant information about it based on its use in the sentence. The fact that few other people know of their existence allows you to assume that "arcane texts" must be rare and be of interest to a few people. Also, the texts are being read by an elderly scholar. So, you can assume that they focus on difficult academic subjects. Sometimes, words can be defined by what they are not. Consider the following sentence: *Ron's fealty to his parents was not shared by Karen, who disobeyed their every command.* Someone who disobeys is not demonstrating *fealty*. So, you can infer that the word means something like *obedience* or *respect*.

Integration of Knowledge and Ideas

FACT AND OPINION

Readers must always be conscious of the distinction between fact and opinion. A fact can be subjected to analysis and can be either proved or disproved. An opinion, on the other hand, is the author's personal thoughts or feelings which may not be alterable by research or evidence. If the author writes that the distance from New York to Boston is about two hundred miles, then he or she is stating a fact. If an author writes that New York is too crowded, then he or she is giving an opinion because there is no objective standard for overpopulation.

An opinion may be indicated by words like *believe*, *think*, or *feel*. Readers must be aware that an opinion may be supported by facts. For instance, the author might give the population density of New York as a reason for an overcrowded population. An opinion supported by fact tends to be more convincing. On the other hand, when authors support their opinions with other opinions, readers should not be persuaded by the argument to any degree.

> **Review Video: <u>Fact or Opinion</u>**
> Visit mometrix.com/academy and enter code: 870899

BIASES AND STEREOTYPES

Every author has a point-of-view, but authors demonstrate a bias when they ignore reasonable counterarguments or distort opposing viewpoints. A bias is evident whenever the author is unfair or inaccurate in his or her presentation. Bias may be intentional or unintentional, and readers should be skeptical of the author's argument. Remember that a biased author may still be correct; however, the author will be correct in spite of his or her bias, not because of the bias. A stereotype is like a bias, yet a stereotype is applied specifically to a group or place. Stereotyping is considered to be particularly abhorrent because the practice promotes negative generalizations about people. Readers should be very cautious of authors who stereotype in their writing. These faulty assumptions typically reveal the author's ignorance and lack of curiosity.

> **Review Video: <u>Bias</u>**
> Visit mometrix.com/academy and enter code: 456336

EVALUATING AN ARGUMENT

Argumentative and persuasive passages take a stand on a debatable issue, seek to explore all sides of the issue, and find the best possible solution. Argumentative and persuasive passages should not be combative or abusive. The word *argument* may remind you of two or more people shouting at each other and walking away in anger. However, an argumentative or persuasive passage should be a calm and reasonable presentation of an author's ideas for others to consider. When an author writes reasonable arguments, his or her goal is not to win or have the last word. Instead, authors want to reveal current understanding of the question at hand and suggest a solution to a problem. The purpose of argument and persuasion in a free society is to reach the best solution.

EVIDENCE

The term **text evidence** refers to information that supports a main point or minor points and can help lead the reader to a conclusion. Information used as text evidence is precise, descriptive, and factual. A main point is often followed by supporting details that provide evidence to back up a claim. For example, a passage may include the claim that winter occurs during opposite months in the Northern and Southern hemispheres. Text evidence based on this claim may include countries

48

where winter occurs in opposite months along with reasons that winter occurs at different times of the year in separate hemispheres (due to the tilt of the Earth as it rotates around the sun).

Evidence needs to be provided that supports the thesis and additional arguments. Most arguments must be supported by facts or statistics. Facts are something that is known with certainty and have been verified by several independent individuals. Examples and illustrations add an emotional component to arguments. With this component, you persuade readers in ways that facts and statistics cannot. The emotional component is effective when used with objective information that can be confirmed.

CREDIBILITY

The text used to support an argument can be the argument's downfall if the text is not credible. A text is **credible**, or believable, when the author is knowledgeable and objective, or unbiased. The author's motivations for writing the text play a critical role in determining the credibility of the text and must be evaluated when assessing that credibility. Reports written about the ozone layer by an environmental scientist and a hairdresser will have a different level of credibility.

APPEAL TO EMOTION

Sometimes, authors will appeal to the reader's emotion in an attempt to persuade or to distract the reader from the weakness of the argument. For instance, the author may try to inspire the pity of the reader by delivering a heart-rending story. An author also might use the bandwagon approach, in which he suggests that his opinion is correct because it is held by the majority. Some authors resort to name-calling, in which insults and harsh words are delivered to the opponent in an attempt to distract. In advertising, a common appeal is the celebrity testimonial, in which a famous person endorses a product. Of course, the fact that a famous person likes something should not really mean anything to the reader. These and other emotional appeals are usually evidence of poor reasoning and a weak argument.

COUNTER ARGUMENTS

When authors give both sides to the argument, they build trust with their readers. As a reader, you should start with an undecided or neutral position. If an author presents only his or her side to the argument, then you will need to be concerned at best.

Building common ground with neutral or opposed readers can be appealing to skeptical readers. Sharing values with undecided readers can allow people to switch positions without giving up what they feel is important. For people who may oppose a position, they need to feel that they can change their minds without betraying who they are as a person. This appeal to having an open mind can be a powerful tool in arguing a position without antagonizing other views. Objections can be countered on a point-by-point basis or in a summary paragraph. Be mindful of how an author points out flaws in counter arguments. If they are unfair to the other side of the argument, then you should lose trust with the author.

PRIMARY SOURCES AND INTERNET SOURCES
PRIMARY SOURCES

When conducting research, it is important to depend on reputable primary sources. A primary source is the documentary evidence closest to the subject being studied. For instance, the primary sources for an essay about penguins would be photographs and recordings of the birds, as well as accounts of people who have studied penguins in person. A secondary source would be a review of a movie about penguins or a book outlining the observations made by others. A primary source should be credible and, if it is on a subject that is still being explored, recent. One way to assess the credibility of a work is to see how often it is mentioned in other books and articles on the same subject. Just by reading the works cited and bibliographies of other books, one can get a sense of what the reliable sources authorities in the field are.

INTERNET SOURCES

The Internet was once considered a poor place to find sources for an essay or article, but its credibility has improved greatly over the years. Still, students need to exercise caution when performing research online. The best sources are those affiliated with established institutions, such as universities, public libraries, and think tanks. Most newspapers are available online, and many of them allow the public to browse their archives. Magazines frequently offer similar services. When obtaining information from an unknown website, however, one must exercise considerably more caution. A website can be considered trustworthy if it is referenced by other sites that are known to be reputable. Also, credible sites tend to be properly maintained and frequently updated. A site is easier to trust when the author provides some information about himself, including some credentials that indicate expertise in the subject matter.

MAKING PREDICTIONS AND DRAWING CONCLUSIONS
PREDICTIONS

A prediction is a guess about what will happen next. Readers constantly make predictions based on what they have read and what they already know. Consider the following sentence: *Staring at the computer screen in shock, Kim blindly reached over for the brimming glass of water on the shelf to her side.* The sentence suggests that Kim is agitated, and that she is not looking at the glass that she is going to pick up. So, a reader might predict that Kim is going to knock over the glass. Of course, not every prediction will be accurate: perhaps Kim will pick the glass up cleanly. Nevertheless, the author has certainly created the expectation that the water might be spilled. Predictions are always subject to revision as the reader acquires more information.

> **Review Video: <u>Predictions</u>**
> Visit mometrix.com/academy and enter code: 437248

FORESHADOWING

Foreshadowing uses hints in a narrative to let the audience anticipate future events in the plot. Foreshadowing can be indicated by a number of literary devices and figures of speech, as well as through dialogue between characters.

DRAWING CONCLUSIONS

In addition to inference and prediction, readers must often **draw conclusions** about the information they have read. When asked for a *conclusion* that may be drawn, look for critical "hedge" phrases, such as *likely, may, can, will often,* among many others. When you are being tested on this knowledge, remember the question that writers insert into these hedge phrases to cover every possibility. Often an answer will be wrong simply because there is no room for exception.

Extreme positive or negative answers (such as always or never) are usually not correct. The reader <u>should not</u> use any outside knowledge that is not gathered from the passage to answer the related questions. Correct answers can be derived straight from the passage.

Writing

Conventions of Standard English

THE EIGHT PARTS OF SPEECH
NOUNS

When you talk about a person, place, thing, or idea, you are talking about nouns. The two main types of nouns are common and proper nouns. Also, nouns can be abstract (i.e., general) or concrete (i.e., specific).

Common nouns are the class or group of people, places, and things (Note: do not capitalize common nouns). Examples of common nouns:

People: boy, girl, worker, manager

Places: school, bank, library, home

Things: dog, cat, truck, car

Proper nouns are the names of specific persons, places, or things (Note: capitalize all proper nouns). Examples of proper nouns:

People: Abraham Lincoln, George Washington, Martin Luther King, Jr.

Places: Los Angeles, New York, Asia

Things: Statue of Liberty, Earth*, Lincoln Memorial

*Note: When you talk about the planet that we live on, you capitalize *Earth*. When you mean the dirt, rocks, or land, you lowercase *earth*.

General nouns are the names of conditions or ideas. **Specific nouns** name people, places, and things that are understood by using your senses.

General nouns:

Condition: beauty, strength

Idea: truth, peace

Specific nouns:

People: baby, friend, father

Places: town, park, city hall

Things: rainbow, cough, apple, silk, gasoline

Collective nouns are the names for a person, place, or thing that may act as a whole. The following are examples of collective nouns: *class, company, dozen, group, herd, team,* and *public*.

PRONOUNS

Pronouns are words that are used to stand in for a noun. A pronoun may be grouped as personal, intensive, relative, interrogative, demonstrative, indefinite, and reciprocal.

Personal: Nominative is the case for nouns and pronouns that are the subject of a sentence. Objective is the case for nouns and pronouns that are an object in a sentence. Possessive is the case for nouns and pronouns that show possession or ownership.

Singular

	Nominative	Objective	Possessive
First Person	I	me	my, mine
Second Person	you	you	your, yours
Third Person	he, she, it	him, her, it	his, her, hers, its

Plural

	Nominative	Objective	Possessive
First Person	we	us	our, ours
Second Person	you	you	your, yours
Third Person	they	them	their, theirs

Intensive: I myself, you yourself, he himself, she herself, the (thing) itself, we ourselves, you yourselves, they themselves

Relative: which, who, whom, whose

Interrogative: what, which, who, whom, whose

Demonstrative: this, that, these, those

Indefinite: all, any, each, everyone, either/neither, one, some, several

Reciprocal: each other, one another

> **Review Video: Nouns and Pronouns**
> Visit mometrix.com/academy and enter code: 312073

VERBS

If you want to write a sentence, then you need a verb in your sentence. Without a verb, you have no sentence. The verb of a sentence explains action or being. In other words, the verb shows the subject's movement or the movement that has been done to the subject.

TRANSITIVE AND INTRANSITIVE VERBS

A transitive verb is a verb whose action (e.g., drive, run, jump) points to a receiver (e.g., car, dog, kangaroo). Intransitive verbs do not point to a receiver of an action. In other words, the action of the verb does not point to a subject or object.

Transitive: He plays the piano. | The piano was played by him.

Intransitive: He plays. | John writes well.

A dictionary will let you know whether a verb is transitive or intransitive. Some verbs can be transitive and intransitive.

ACTION VERBS AND LINKING VERBS

An action verb is a verb that shows what the subject is doing in a sentence. In other words, an action verb shows action. A sentence can be complete with one word: an action verb. Linking verbs are intransitive verbs that show a condition (i.e., the subject is described but does no action).

Linking verbs link the subject of a sentence to a noun or pronoun, or they link a subject with an adjective. You always need a verb if you want a complete sentence. However, linking verbs are not able to complete a sentence.

Common linking verbs include *appear, be, become, feel, grow, look, seem, smell, sound,* and *taste.* However, any verb that shows a condition and has a noun, pronoun, or adjective that describes the subject of a sentence is a linking verb.

Action: He sings. | Run! | Go! | I talk with him every day. | She reads.

Linking:

Incorrect: I feel.

Correct: I am John. | I smell roses. | I feel tired.

Note: Some verbs are followed by words that look like prepositions, but they are a part of the verb and a part of the verb's meaning. These are known as phrasal verbs and examples include *call off, look up,* and *drop off.*

> **Review Video: Action Verbs and Linking Verbs**
> Visit mometrix.com/academy and enter code: 743142

VOICE

Transitive verbs come in active or passive voice. If the subject does an action or receives the action of the verb, then you will know whether a verb is active or passive. When the subject of the sentence is doing the action, the verb is active voice. When the subject receives the action, the verb is passive voice.

Active: Jon drew the picture. (The subject *Jon* is doing the action of *drawing a picture.*)

Passive: The picture is drawn by Jon. (The subject *picture* is receiving the action from Jon.)

VERB TENSES

A verb tense shows the different form of a verb to point to the time of an action. The present and past tense are shown by changing the verb's form. An action in the present *I talk* can change form for the past: *I talked.* However, for the other tenses, an auxiliary (i.e., helping) verb is needed to show the change in form. These helping verbs include *am, are, is | have, has, had | was, were, will* (or *shall*).

Present: I talk	Present perfect: I have talked
Past: I talked	Past perfect: I had talked
Future: I will talk	Future perfect: I will have talked

Present: The action happens at the current time.

Example: He *walks* to the store every morning.

To show that something is happening right now, use the progressive present tense: I *am walking*.

Past: The action happened in the past.

Example: He *walked* to the store an hour ago.

Future: The action is going to happen later.

Example: I *will walk* to the store tomorrow.

Present perfect: The action started in the past and continues into the present.

Example: I *have walked* to the store three times today.

Past perfect: The second action happened in the past. The first action came before the second.

Example: Before I walked to the store (Action 2), I *had walked* to the library (Action 1).

Future perfect: An action that uses the past and the future. In other words, the action is complete before a future moment.

Example: When she comes for the supplies (future moment), I *will have walked* to the store (action completed in the past).

Review Video: <u>Present Perfect, Past Perfect, and Future Perfect Verb Tenses</u>
Visit mometrix.com/academy and enter code: 269472

CONJUGATING VERBS

When you need to change the form of a verb, you are conjugating a verb. The key parts of a verb are first person singular, present tense (dream); first person singular, past tense (dreamed); and the past participle (dreamed). Note: the past participle needs a helping verb to make a verb tense. For example, I *have dreamed* of this day. | I *am dreaming* of this day.

Present Tense: Active Voice

	Singular	**Plural**
First Person	I dream	We dream
Second Person	You dream	You dream
Third Person	He, she, it dreams	They dream

MOOD

There are three moods in English: the indicative, the imperative, and the subjunctive.

The **indicative mood** is used for facts, opinions, and questions.

Fact: You can do this.

Opinion: I think that you can do this.

Question: Do you know that you can do this?

The **imperative** is used for orders or requests.

Order: You are going to do this!

Request: Will you do this for me?

The **subjunctive mood** is for wishes and statements that go against fact.

Wish: I wish that I were going to do this.

Statement against fact: If I were you, I would do this. (This goes against fact because I am not you. You have the chance to do this, and I do not have the chance.)

The mood that causes trouble for most people is the subjunctive mood. If you have trouble with any of the moods, then be sure to practice.

ADJECTIVES

An adjective is a word that is used to modify a noun or pronoun. An adjective answers a question: *Which one?*, *What kind of?*, or *How many?*. Usually, adjectives come before the words that they modify.

Which one?: The *third* suit is my favorite.

What kind?: The *navy blue* suit is my favorite.

How many?: Can I look over the *four* neckties for the suit?

ARTICLES

Articles are adjectives that are used to mark nouns. There are only three: the definite (i.e., limited or fixed amount) article *the*, and the indefinite (i.e., no limit or fixed amount) articles *a* and *an*. Note: *An* comes before words that start with a vowel sound (i.e., vowels include *a, e, i, o, u*, and *y*). For example, Are you going to get an **u**mbrella?

Definite: I lost *the* bottle that belongs to me.

Indefinite: Does anyone have *a* bottle to share?

COMPARISON WITH ADJECTIVES

Some adjectives are relative and other adjectives are absolute. Adjectives that are relative can show the comparison between things. Adjectives that are absolute can show comparison. However, they show comparison in a different way. Let's say that you are reading two books. You think that one book is perfect, and the other book is not exactly perfect. It is <u>not</u> possible for the book to be more perfect than the other. Either you think that the book is perfect, or you think that the book is not perfect.

The adjectives that are relative will show the different degrees of something or someone to something else or someone else. The three degrees of adjectives include positive, comparative, and superlative.

The positive degree is the normal form of an adjective.

Example: This work is *difficult*. | She is *smart*.

The comparative degree compares one person or thing to another person or thing.

Example: This work is *more difficult* than your work. | She is *smarter* than me.

The superlative degree compares more than two people or things.

Example: This is the *most difficult* work of my life. | She is the *smartest* lady in school.

ADVERBS

An adverb is a word that is used to modify a verb, adjective, or another adverb. Usually, adverbs answer one of these questions: *When?*, *Where?*, *How?*, and *Why?* . The negatives *not* and *never* are known as adverbs. Adverbs that modify adjectives or other adverbs strengthen or weaken the words that they modify.

Examples:

He walks quickly through the crowd.

The water flows smoothly on the rocks.

Note: While many adverbs end in -*ly*, you need to remember that not all adverbs end in -*ly*. Also, some words that end in -*ly* are adjectives, not adverbs. Some examples include: *early, friendly, holy, lonely, silly*, and *ugly*. To know if a word that ends in -*ly* is an adjective or adverb, you can check whether it answers one of the adjective questions or one of the adverb questions.

Examples:

He is *never* angry.

You talk *too* loudly.

COMPARISON WITH ADVERBS

The rules for comparing adverbs are the same as the rules for adjectives.

The positive degree is the standard form of an adverb.

Example: He arrives soon. | She speaks softly to her friends.

The comparative degree compares one person or thing to another person or thing.

Example: He arrives sooner than Sarah. | She speaks more softly than him.

The superlative degree compares more than two people or things.

Example: He arrives soonest of the group. | She speaks most softly of any of her friends.

PREPOSITIONS

A preposition is a word placed before a noun or pronoun that shows the relationship between an object and another word in the sentence.

Common Prepositions:

about	before	duringon	under
after	beneath	for	over	until
againstbetweenfrom	past	up
among	beyond	in	throughwith
aroundby	of	to	within
at	down	off	toward	without

Examples:

The napkin is *in* the drawer.

The Earth rotates *around* the Sun.

The needle is *beneath* the haystack.

Can you find me *among* the words?

Review Video: What is a Preposition?
Visit mometrix.com/academy and enter code: 946763

CONJUNCTIONS

Conjunctions join words, phrases, or clauses, and they show the connection between the joined pieces. There are coordinating conjunctions that connect equal parts of sentences. Correlative conjunctions show the connection between pairs. Subordinating conjunctions join subordinate (i.e., dependent) clauses with independent clauses.

COORDINATING CONJUNCTIONS

The coordinating conjunctions include: *and, but, yet, or, nor, for,* and *so*

Examples:

The rock was small, but it was heavy.

She drove in the night, and he drove in the day.

CORRELATIVE CONJUNCTIONS

The correlative conjunctions are: either...or | neither...nor | not only... but also

Examples:

Either you are coming, or you are staying. | He ran not only three miles, but also swam 200 yards.

Review Video: Coordinating and Correlative Conjunctions
Visit mometrix.com/academy and enter code: 390329

SUBORDINATING CONJUNCTIONS

Common subordinating conjunctions include:

after	since	whenever
although	so that	where
because	unless	wherever
before	until	whether
in order that	when	while

Examples:

I am hungry *because* I did not eat breakfast.

He went home *when* everyone left.

Review Video: Subordinating Conjunctions
Visit mometrix.com/academy and enter code: 958913

INTERJECTIONS

An interjection is a word for exclamation (i.e., great amount of feeling) that is used alone or as a piece to a sentence. Often, they are used at the beginning of a sentence for an introduction. Sometimes, they can be used in the middle of a sentence to show a change in thought or attitude. Common Interjections: Hey! | Oh,... | Ouch! | Please! | Wow!

Punctuation

END PUNCTUATION

PERIODS

Use a period to end all sentences except direct questions, exclamations, and questions.

DECLARATIVE SENTENCE

A declarative sentence gives information or makes a statement.

Examples: I can fly a kite. | The plane left two hours ago.

IMPERATIVE SENTENCE

An imperative sentence gives an order or command.

Examples: You are coming with me. | Bring me that note.

QUESTION MARKS

Question marks should be used following a direct question. A polite request can be followed by a period instead of a question mark.

Direct Question: What is for lunch today? | How are you? | Why is that the answer?

Polite Requests:

Can you please send me the item tomorrow? | Will you please walk with me on the track?

EXCLAMATION MARKS

Exclamation marks are used after a word group or sentence that shows much feeling or has special importance. Exclamation marks should not be overused. They are saved for proper exclamatory interjections.

Examples: We're going to the finals! | You have a beautiful car! | That's crazy!

SPECIAL NOTE

PERIODS FOR ABBREVIATIONS

An abbreviation is a shortened form of a word or phrase.

Examples: 3 P.M. | 2 A.M. | Mr. Jones | Mrs. Stevens | Dr. Smith | Bill Jr. | Pennsylvania Ave.

COMMAS

The comma is a punctuation mark that can help you understand connections in a sentence. Not every sentence needs a comma. However, if a sentence needs a comma, you need to put it in the right place. A comma in the wrong place (or an absent comma) will make a sentence's meaning unclear. These are some of the rules for commas:

1. Use a comma before a coordinating conjunction joining independent clauses
   Example: Bob caught three fish, and I caught two fish.
2. Use a comma after an introductory phrase or an adverbial clause
   Examples:
   After the final out, we went to a restaurant to celebrate.

Studying the stars, I was surprised at the beauty of the sky.

3. Use a comma between items in a series.

    Example: I will bring the turkey, the pie, and the coffee.

4. Use a comma between coordinate adjectives not joined with *and*

    Incorrect: The kind, brown dog followed me home.
    Correct: The *kind, loyal* dog followed me home.
    Not all adjectives are coordinate (i.e., equal or parallel). There are two simple ways to know if your adjectives are coordinate. One, you can join the adjectives with *and*: *The kind and loyal dog.* Two, you can change the order of the adjectives: *The loyal, kind dog.*

5. Use commas for interjections and after *yes* and *no* responses

    Examples:

        Interjection: Oh, I had no idea. | Wow, you know how to play this game.
        Yes and No: *Yes,* I heard you. | *No,* I cannot come tomorrow.

6. Use commas to separate nonessential modifiers and nonessential appositives

    Examples:

        Nonessential Modifier: John Frank, who is coaching the team, was promoted today.
        Nonessential Appositive: Thomas Edison, an American inventor, was born in Ohio.

7. Use commas to set off nouns of direct address, interrogative tags, and contrast

    Examples:

        Direct Address: You, *John,* are my only hope in this moment.
        Interrogative Tag: This is the last time, *correct*?
        Contrast: You are my friend, *not my enemy.*

8. Use commas with dates, addresses, geographical names, and titles

    Examples:

        Date: *July 4, 1776,* is an important date to remember.
        Address: He is meeting me at *456 Delaware Avenue, Washington, D.C.,* tomorrow morning.
        Geographical Name: *Paris, France,* is my favorite city.
        Title: John Smith, *Ph. D.,* will be visiting your class today.

9. Use commas to separate expressions like *he said* and *she said* if they come between a sentence of a quote

    Examples:

        "I want you to know," he began, "that I always wanted the best for you."
        "You can start," Jane said, "with an apology."

Review Video: Commas
Visit mometrix.com/academy and enter code: 786797

SEMICOLONS

The semicolon is used to connect major sentence pieces of equal value. Some rules for semicolons include:

1. Use a semicolon between closely connected independent clauses that are not connected with a coordinating conjunction.

    Examples:

She is outside; we are inside.
You are right; we should go with your plan.

2. Use a semicolon between independent clauses linked with a transitional word.

   Examples:

   I think that we can agree on this; *however,* I am not sure about my friends.
   You are looking in the wrong places; *therefore,* you will not find what you need.

3. Use a semicolon between items in a series that has internal punctuation.

   Example: I have visited New York, New York; Augusta, Maine; and Baltimore, Maryland.

> **Review Video: Semicolon Usage**
> Visit mometrix.com/academy and enter code: 370605

COLONS

The colon is used to call attention to the words that follow it. A colon must come after an independent clause. The rules for colons are as follows:

1. Use a colon after an independent clause to make a list

   Example: I want to learn many languages: Spanish, French, German, and Italian.

2. Use a colon for explanations or to give a quote

   Examples:

   Quote: The man started with an idea: "We are able to do more than we imagine."
   Explanation: There is one thing that stands out on your resume: responsibility.

3. Use a colon after the greeting in a formal letter, to show hours and minutes, and to separate a title and subtitle

   Examples:

   Greeting in a formal letter: Dear Sir: | To Whom It May Concern:
   Time: It is 3:14 P.M.
   Title: The essay is titled "America: A Short Introduction to a Modern Country"

PARENTHESES

Parentheses are used for additional information. Also, they can be used to put labels for letters or numbers in a series. Parentheses should not be used very often. If they are overused, parentheses can be a distraction instead of a help.

Examples:

Extra Information: The rattlesnake (see Image 2) is a dangerous snake of North and South America.

Series: Include in the email (1) your name, (2) your address, and (3) your question for the author.

QUOTATION MARKS

Use quotation marks to close off direct quotations of a person's spoken or written words. Do not use quotation marks around indirect quotations. An indirect quotation gives someone's message without using the person's exact words. Use single quotation marks to close off a quotation inside a quotation.

Direct Quote: Nancy said, "I am waiting for Henry to arrive."

Indirect Quote: Henry said that he is going to be late to the meeting.

Quote inside a Quote: The teacher asked, "Has everyone read 'The Gift of the Magi'?"

Quotation marks should be used around the titles of short works: newspaper and magazine articles, poems, short stories, songs, television episodes, radio programs, and subdivisions of books or web sites.

Examples:

"Rip van Winkle" (short story by Washington Irving)

"O Captain! My Captain!" (poem by Walt Whitman)

Quotation marks may be used to set off words that are being used in a different way from a dictionary definition. Also, they can be used to highlight irony.

Examples:

The boss warned Frank that he was walking on "thin ice."

(Frank is not walking on real ice. Instead, Frank is being warned to avoid mistakes.)

The teacher thanked the young man for his "honesty."

(Honesty and truth are not always the same thing. In this example, the quotation marks around *honesty* show that the teacher does not believe the young man's explanation.)

Review Video: Quotation Marks
Visit mometrix.com/academy and enter code: 884918

Note: Periods and commas are put inside quotation marks. Colons and semicolons are put outside the quotation marks. Question marks and exclamation points are placed inside quotation marks when they are part of a quote. When the question or exclamation mark goes with the whole sentence, the mark is left outside of the quotation marks.

Examples:

Period and comma: We read "The Gift of the Magi," "The Skylight Room," and "The Cactus."

Semicolon: They watched "The Nutcracker"; then, they went home.

Exclamation mark that is a part of a quote: The crowd cheered, "Victory!"

Question mark that goes with the whole sentence: Is your favorite short story "The Tell-Tale Heart"?

APOSTROPHES

An apostrophe is used to show possession or the deletion of letters in contractions. An apostrophe is not needed with the possessive pronouns *his, hers, its, ours, theirs, whose*, and *yours*.

Singular Nouns: David's car | a book's theme | my brother's board game

Plural Nouns with -*s*: the scissors' handle | boys' basketball

Plural Nouns without -s: Men's department | the people's adventure

HYPHEN

The hyphen is used to separate compound words. The following are the rules for hyphens:

1. Compound numbers come with a hyphen

   Example: This team needs *twenty-five* points to win the game.

2. Fractions need a hyphen if they are used as an adjective

   Correct: The recipe says that we need a *three-fourths* cup of butter.
   Incorrect: *One-fourth* of the road is under construction.

3. Compound words used as adjectives that come before a noun need a hyphen

   Correct: The *well-fed* dog took a nap.
   Incorrect: The dog was *well-fed* for his nap.

4. To avoid confusion with some words, use a hyphen

   Examples: semi-irresponsible | Re-collect |Re-claim

Note: This is not a complete set of the rules for hyphens. A dictionary is the best tool for knowing if a compound word needs a hyphen.

DASHES

Dashes are used to show a break or a change in thought in a sentence or to act as parentheses in a sentence. When typing, use two hyphens to make a dash. Do not put a space before or after the dash. The following are the rules for dashes:

1. To set off parenthetical statements or an appositive that has internal punctuation.

   Example: The three trees—oak, pine, and magnolia—are coming on a truck tomorrow.

2. To show a break or change in tone or thought.

   Example: The first question—how silly of me—does not have a correct answer.

ELLIPSIS MARKS

The ellipsis mark has three periods (...) to show when words have been removed from a quotation. If a full sentence or more is removed from a quoted passage, you need to use four periods to show the removed text and the end punctuation mark. The ellipsis mark should not be used at the beginning of a quotation. Also, the ellipsis should not be used at the end of a quotation. The exception is when some words have been deleted from the end of the final sentence.

The following sentence provides an example:

"...Then he picked up the groceries...paid for them...later he went home...."

BRACKETS

There are two main ways to use brackets:

1. When you need to place parentheses inside of parentheses, you use brackets instead of parentheses.

    Example: The hero of this story, Paul Revere (a silversmith and industrialist [see Ch. 4]), rode through towns of Massachusetts to warn of advancing British troops.

2. You can use brackets when you need to add material that is being quoted.

    Example: The father explained, "My children are planning to attend my alma mater [State University]."

Improving Sentences

CAPITALIZATION

The rules for capitalization are:

1. Capitalize the first word of a sentence and the first word in a direct quotation

    Examples:

    > First Word: *Football* is my favorite sport.
    > Direct Quote: She asked, "*What* is your name?"

2. Capitalize proper nouns and adjectives that come from proper nouns

    Examples:

    > Proper Noun: My parents are from *Europe.*
    > Adjective from Proper Noun: My father is *British,* and my mother is *Italian.*

3. Capitalize the names of days, months, and holidays

    Examples:

    > Day: Everyone needs to be here on *Wednesday.*
    > Month: I am so excited for *December.*
    > Holiday: *Independence Day* comes every July.

4. Capitalize the names on a compass for specific areas, not when they give direction

    Examples:

    > Specific Area: James is from the *West.*
    > Direction: After three miles, turn *south* toward the highway.

5. Capitalize each word in a title (Note: Articles, prepositions, and conjunctions are not capitalized unless they are the first or last word in the title.)

    Examples:

    > Titles: <u>*Romeo and Juliet*</u> is a beautiful drama on love.
    > Incorrect: <u>*The Taming Of The Shrew*</u> is my favorite. (Remember that internal prepositions and articles are not capitalized.)

    Note: Books, movies, plays (more than one act), newspapers, magazines, and long musical pieces are put in italics. The two examples of Shakespeare's plays are underlined to show their use as an example.

SUBJECTS AND PREDICATES

SUBJECTS

The *subject* of a sentence names who or what the sentence is about. The complete subject is composed of the simple subject and all of its modifiers. To find the complete subject, ask *Who* or *What* and insert the verb to complete the question. The answer is the complete subject. To find the simple subject, remove all of the modifiers in the complete subject.

Examples:

The small red car is the one that he wants for Christmas.
(The complete subject is *the small red car.*)

The young artist is coming over for dinner.
(The complete subject is *the young artist.*)

In imperative sentences, the verb's subject is understood, but not actually present in the sentence. Although the subject ordinarily comes before the verb, in sentences that begin with *There are* or *There was*, the subject follows the verb. The ability to recognize the subject of a sentence helps in editing a variety of problems, such as sentence fragments and subject-verb agreement, as well as the using the correct pronouns.

> **Review Video: Subjects**
> Visit mometrix.com/academy and enter code: 444771

Direct:

John knows the way to the park.
(Who knows the way to the park? Answer: John)

The cookies need ten more minutes.
(What needs ten minutes? Answer: The cookies)

By five o' clock, Bill will need to leave.
(Who needs to leave? Answer: Bill)

Remember: The subject can come after the verb.

There are five letters on the table for him.
(What is on the table? Answer: Five letters)

There were coffee and doughnuts in the house.
(What was in the house? Answer: Coffee and doughnuts)

Implied:

Go to the post office for me.
(Who is going to the post office? Answer: You are.)

Come and sit with me, please?
(Who needs to come and sit? Answer: You do.)

PREDICATES

In a sentence, you always have a predicate and a subject. A predicate is what remains when you have found the subject. The subject tells what the sentence is about, and the predicate explains or describes the subject. Think about the sentence: *He sings*. In this sentence, we have a subject (He) and a predicate (sings). This is all that is needed for a sentence to be complete. Would we like more information? Of course, we would like to know more. However, if this all the information that you are given, you have a complete sentence.

Now, let's look at another sentence:

John and Jane sing on Tuesday nights at the dance hall.

What is the subject of this sentence?
Answer: John and Jane.

What is the predicate of this sentence?
Answer: Everything else in the sentence besides John and Jane.

SUBJECT-VERB AGREEMENT

Verbs agree with their subjects in number. In other words, singular subjects need singular verbs. Plural subjects need plural verbs. Singular is for one person, place, or thing. Plural is for more than one person, place, or thing. Subjects and verbs must also agree in person: first, second, or third. The present tense ending *-s* is used on a verb if its subject is third person singular; otherwise, the verb takes no ending.

Review Video: <u>Subject Verb Agreement</u>
Visit mometrix.com/academy and enter code: 479190

NUMBER AGREEMENT EXAMPLES:

Single Subject and Verb: *Dan calls home.*
(Dan is one person. So, the singular verb *calls* is needed.)

Plural Subject and Verb: *Dan and Bob call home.*
(More than one person needs the plural verb *call*.)

PERSON AGREEMENT EXAMPLES:

First Person: I *am* walking.

Second Person: You *are* walking.

Third Person: He *is* walking.

PROBLEMS WITH SUBJECT-VERB AGREEMENT

WORDS BETWEEN SUBJECT AND VERB

The joy of my life returns home tonight.
(**Singular Subject**: joy. **Singular Verb**: returns)

The phrase *of my life* does not influence the verb *returns*.

The question that still remains unanswered is "Who are you?"
(**Singular Subject**: question. **Singular Verb**: is)

Don't let the phrase "*that still remains...*" trouble you. The subject *question* goes with *is*.

COMPOUND SUBJECTS

You and Jon are invited to come to my house.
(**Plural Subject**: You and Jon. **Plural Verb**: are)

The pencil and paper belong to me.
(**Plural Subject**: pencil and paper. **Plural Verb**: belong)

SUBJECTS JOINED BY OR AND NOR

Today or tomorrow is the day.
(**Subject**: Today / tomorrow. **Verb**: is)

Stan or Phil wants to read the book.
(**Subject**: Stan / Phil. **Verb**: wants)

Neither the books nor the *pen is* on the desk.
(**Subject**: Books / Pen. **Verb**: is)

Either the blanket or *pillows arrive* this afternoon.
(**Subject**: Blanket / Pillows. **Verb**: arrive)

Note: Singular subjects that are joined with the conjunction *or* need a singular verb. However, when one subject is singular and another is plural, you make the verb agree with the closer subject. The example about books and the pen has a singular verb because the pen (singular subject) is closer to the verb.

INDEFINITE PRONOUNS: EITHER, NEITHER, AND EACH

Is either of you ready for the game?
(**Singular Subject**: Either. **Singular Verb**: is)

Each man, woman, and child is unique.
(**Singular Subject**: Each. **Singular Verb**: is)

THE ADJECTIVE EVERY AND COMPOUNDS: EVERYBODY, EVERYONE, ANYBODY, ANYONE

Every day passes faster than the last.
(**Singular Subject**: Every day. **Singular Verb**: passes)

Anybody is welcome to bring a tent.
(**Singular Subject**: Anybody. **Singular Verb**: is)

COLLECTIVE NOUNS

The family eats at the restaurant every Friday night.
(The members of the family are one at the restaurant.)

The team are leaving for their homes after the game.
(The members of the team are leaving as individuals to go to their own homes.)

WHO, WHICH, AND THAT AS SUBJECT

This is the man who is helping me today.

He is a good man who serves others before himself.

This painting that is hung over the couch is very beautiful.

PLURAL FORM AND SINGULAR MEANING

Some nouns that are singular in meaning but plural in form: news, mathematics, physics, and economics.

The news is coming on now.

Mathematics is my favorite class.

Some nouns that are plural in meaning: athletics, gymnastics, scissors, and pants.

Do these pants come with a shirt?

The scissors are for my project.

Note: Look to your dictionary for help when you aren't sure whether a noun with a plural form has a singular or plural meaning.

Addition, Multiplication, Subtraction, and Division are normally singular.

One plus one is two.

Three times three is nine.

COMPLEMENTS

A complement is a noun, pronoun, or adjective that is used to give more information about the verb in the sentence.

DIRECT OBJECTS

A direct object is a noun that takes or receives the action of a verb. Remember: a complete sentence does not need a direct object. A sentence needs only a subject and a verb. When you are looking for a direct object, find the verb and ask *who* or *what*.

Example: I took the blanket. (Who or what did I take? *The blanket*)

Jane read books. (Who or what does Jane read? *Books*)

INDIRECT OBJECTS

An indirect object is a word or group of words that show how an action had an influence on someone or something. If there is an indirect object in a sentence, then you always have a direct object in the sentence. When you are looking for the indirect object, find the verb and ask *to/for whom or what*.

Examples: We taught the old dog a new trick.
(To/For Whom or What was taught? *The old dog*)

I gave them a math lesson.
(To/For Whom or What was given? *Them*)

> **Review Video: <u>Direct and Indirect Objects</u>**
> Visit mometrix.com/academy and enter code: 817385

<u>Predicate Nouns</u> are nouns that modify the subject and finish linking verbs.

Example: My father is a lawyer.
Father is the subject. Lawyer is the predicate noun.

<u>Predicate Adjectives</u> are adjectives that modify the subject and finish linking verbs.

Example: Your mother is patient.
Mother is the subject. Patient is the predicate adjective.

PRONOUN USAGE

Pronoun-antecedent agreement – The antecedent is the noun that has been replaced by a pronoun. A pronoun and the antecedent agree when they are singular or plural.

Singular agreement: *John* came into town, and *he* played for us.
(The word *He* replaces *John*.)

Plural agreement: *John and Rick* came into town, and *they* played for us.
(The word *They* replaces *John* and *Rick*.)

To know the correct pronoun for a compound subject, try each pronoun separately with the verb.
Your knowledge of pronouns will tell you which one is correct.

Example: Bob and (I, me) will be going.
(Answer: Bob and I will be going.)

Test: (1) *I will be going* or (2) *Me will be going*. The second choice cannot be correct because *me* is
not used as a subject of a sentence. Instead, *me* is used as an object.

When a pronoun is used with a noun immediately following (as in "we boys"), try the sentence
without the added noun.

Example: (We/Us) boys played football last year.
(Answer: We boys played football last year.)

Test: (1) *We* played football last year or (2) *Us* played football last year. Again, the second choice
cannot be correct because *us* is not used as a subject of a sentence. Instead, *us* is used as an object.

Pronoun reference – A pronoun should point clearly to the antecedent. Here is how a pronoun
reference can be unhelpful if it is not directly stated or puzzling.

Unhelpful: Ron and Jim went to the store, and he bought soda.
(Who bought soda? Ron or Jim?)

Helpful: Jim went to the store, and he bought soda.
(The sentence is clear. Jim bought the soda.)

Personal pronouns – Some pronouns change their form by their placement in a sentence. A pronoun
that is a subject in a sentence comes in the subjective case. Pronouns that serve as objects appear
in the objective case. Finally, the pronouns that are used as possessives appear in the possessive
case.

Subjective case: *He* is coming to the show.
(The pronoun *He* is the subject of the sentence.)

Objective case: Josh drove *him* to the airport.
(The pronoun *him* is the object of the sentence.)

Possessive case: The flowers are *mine*.
(The pronoun *mine* shows ownership of the flowers.)

Who or whom – *Who*, a subjective-case pronoun, can be used as a subject. *Whom*, an objective case
pronoun, can be used as an object. The words *who* and *whom* are common in subordinate clauses
or in questions.

71

Subject: He knows who wants to come.
(*Who* is the subject of the verb *wants*.)

Object: He knows whom we want at the party.
(*Whom* is the object of *we want*.)

CLAUSES

There are two groups of clauses: independent and dependent. Unlike phrases, a clause has a subject and a verb. So, what is the difference between a clause that is independent and one that is dependent? An independent clause gives a complete thought. A dependent clause does not share a complete thought. Instead, a dependent clause has a subject and a verb, but it needs an independent clause. Subordinate (i.e., dependent) clauses look like sentences. They may have a subject, a verb, and objects or complements. They are used within sentences as adverbs, adjectives, or nouns.

Examples:

Independent Clause: I am running outside.
(The sentence has a subject *I* and a verb *am running*.)

Dependent Clause: I am running <u>because I want to stay in shape</u>.

The clause *I am running* is an independent clause. The underlined clause is dependent. Remember: a dependent clause does not give a complete thought. Think about the dependent clause: *because I want to stay in shape*.

Without any other information, you think: So, you want to stay in shape. What are you are doing to stay in shape? Answer: *I am running*.

TYPES OF DEPENDENT CLAUSES

An **adjective clause** is a dependent clause that modifies nouns and pronouns. Adjective clauses begin with a relative pronoun (*who, whose, whom, which,* and *that*) or a relative adverb (*where, when,* and *why*). Also, adjective clauses come after the noun that the clause needs to explain or rename. This is done to have a clear connection to the independent clause.

Examples:

I learned the reason *why I won the award.*

This is the place *where I started my first job.*

An adjective clause can be an essential or nonessential clause. An essential clause is very important to the sentence. Essential clauses explain or define a person or thing. Nonessential clauses give more information about a person or thing. However, they are not necessary to the sentence.

Examples:

Essential: A person *who works hard at first* can rest later in life.

Nonessential: Neil Armstrong, *who walked on the moon*, is my hero.

An **adverb clause** is a dependent clause that modifies verbs, adjectives, and other adverbs. To show a clear connection to the independent clause, put the adverb clause immediately before or after the independent clause. An adverb clause can start with *after, although, as, as if, before, because, if, since, so, so that, unless, when, where,* or *while.*

Examples:

When you walked outside, I called the manager.

I want to go with you *unless you want to stay.*

A **noun clause** is a dependent clause that can be used as a subject, object, or complement. Noun clauses can begin with *how, that, what, whether, which, who,* or *why*. These words can also come with an adjective clause. Remember that the entire clause makes a noun or an adjective clause, not the word that starts a clause. So, be sure to look for more than the word that begins the clause. To show a clear connection to the independent clause, be sure that a noun clause comes after the verb. The exception is when the noun clause is the subject of the sentence.

Examples:

The fact *that you were alone* alarms me.

What you learn from each other depends on your honesty with others.

PHRASES

A phrase is not a complete sentence. So, a phrase cannot be a statement and cannot give a complete thought. Instead, a phrase is a group of words that can be used as a noun, adjective, or adverb in a sentence. Phrases strengthen sentences by adding explanation or renaming something.

Prepositional Phrases – A phrase that can be found in many sentences is the prepositional phrase. A prepositional phrase begins with a preposition and ends with a noun or pronoun that is used as an object. Normally, the prepositional phrase works as an adjective or an adverb.

Examples:

The picnic is *on the blanket.*

I am sick *with a fever* today.

Among the many flowers, a four-leaf clover was found by John.

VERBALS AND VERBAL PHRASES

A verbal looks like a verb, but it is not used as a verb. Instead, a verbal is used as a noun, adjective, or adverb. Be careful with verbals. They do not replace a verb in a sentence.

Correct: Walk a mile daily.

(*Walk* is the verb of this sentence. As in, "*You* walk a mile daily.")

Incorrect: To walk a mile.

(*To walk* is a type of verbal. But, verbals cannot be a verb for a sentence.)

A verbal phrase is a verb form that does not function as the verb of a clause. There are three major types of verbal phrases: participial, gerund, and infinitive phrases.

PARTICIPLES

A participle is a verbal that is used as an adjective. The present participle always ends with *-ing*. Past participles end with *-d, -ed, -n,* or *-t.*

Examples: Verb: *dance* | Present Participle: *dancing* | Past Participle: *danced*

Participial phrases are made of a participle and any complements or modifiers. Often, they come right after the noun or pronoun that they modify.

Examples:

Shipwrecked on an island, the boys started to fish for food.

Having been seated for five hours, we got out of the car to stretch our legs.

Praised for their work, the group accepted the first-place trophy.

GERUNDS

A gerund is a verbal that is used as a noun. Gerunds can be found by looking for their *-ing* endings. However, you need to be careful that you have found a gerund, not a present participle. Since gerunds are nouns, they can be used as a subject of a sentence and the object of a verb or preposition.

Gerund Phrases are built around present participles (i.e., *-ing* endings to verbs) and they are always used as nouns. The gerund phrase has a gerund and any complements or modifiers.

Examples:

We want to be known for *teaching the poor*. (Object of Preposition)

Coaching this team is the best job of my life. (Subject)

We like *practicing our songs* in the basement. (Object of the verb: *like*)

INFINITIVES

An infinitive is a verbal that can be used as a noun, an adjective, or an adverb. An infinitive is made of the basic form of a verb with the word *to* coming before the verb.

Infinitive Phrases are made of an infinitive and all complements and modifiers. They are used as nouns, adjectives, or adverbs.

Examples:

To join the team is my goal in life. (Noun)

The animals have enough food *to eat for the night*. (Adjective)

People lift weights *to exercise their muscles*. (Adverb)

APPOSITIVE PHRASES

An appositive is a word or phrase that is used to explain or rename nouns or pronouns. In a sentence they can be noun phrases, prepositional phrases, gerund phrases, or infinitive phrases.

Examples:

Terriers, *hunters at heart*, have been dressed up to look like lap dogs.

(The phrase *hunters at heart* renames the noun *terriers*.)

His plan, *to save and invest his money*, was proven as a safe approach.

(The italicized infinitive phrase renames the plan.)

Appositive phrases can be essential or nonessential. An appositive phrase is essential if the person, place, or thing being described or renamed is too general.

Essential: Two Founding Fathers George Washington and Thomas Jefferson served as presidents.

Nonessential: George Washington and Thomas Jefferson, two Founding Fathers, served as presidents.

ABSOLUTE PHRASES

An absolute phrase is a phrase with a participle that comes after a noun. The absolute phrase is never the subject of a sentence. Also, the phrase does not explain or add to the meaning of a word in a sentence. Absolute phrases are used independently from the rest of the sentence. However, they are still a phrase, and phrases cannot give a complete thought.

Examples:

The alarm ringing, he pushed the snooze button.

The music paused, she continued to dance through the crowd.

Note: Appositive and absolute phrases can be confusing in sentences. So, don't be discouraged if you have a difficult time with them.

MODES OF SENTENCE PATTERNS

Sentence patterns fall into five common modes with some exceptions. They are:

- Subject + linking verb + subject complement
- Subject + transitive verb + direct object
- Subject + transitive verb + indirect object + direct object
- Subject + transitive verb + direct object + object complement
- Subject + intransitive verb

Common exceptions to these patterns are questions and commands, sentences with delayed subjects, and passive transformations.

TYPES OF SENTENCES

For a sentence to be complete, it must have a subject and a verb or predicate. A complete sentence will express a complete thought, otherwise it is known as a fragment. An example of a fragment is:

As the clock struck midnight. A complete sentence would be: *As the clock struck midnight, she ran home.* The types of sentences are declarative, imperative, interrogative, and exclamatory.

A declarative sentence states a fact and ends with a period. The following is an example:

The football game starts at seven o'clock.

An imperative sentence tells someone to do something and ends with a period. The following is an example:

Go to the store and buy milk.

An interrogative sentence asks a question and ends with a question mark. The following is an example:

Are you going to the game on Friday?

An exclamatory sentence shows strong emotion and ends with an exclamation point. The following is an example:

I can't believe we won the game!

SENTENCE STRUCTURES

The four major types of sentence structure are:

1. Simple Sentences – Simple sentences have one independent clause with no subordinate clauses. A simple sentence can have compound elements (e.g., a compound subject or verb).

   Examples:

   > Judy watered the lawn. (Singular Subject & Singular Predicate)
   > Judy and Alan watered the lawn. (Compound Subject: Judy and Alan)

2. Compound Sentences – Compound sentences have two or more independent clauses with no dependent clauses. Usually, the independent clauses are joined with a comma and a coordinating conjunction, or they can be joined with a semicolon.

   Example:

   > The time has come, and we are ready.
   > I woke up at dawn; then I went outside to watch the sun rise.

3. Complex Sentences – A complex sentence has one independent clause and one or more dependent clauses.

   Examples:

   > Although he had the flu, Harry went to work.
   > Marcia got married after she finished college.

4. Compound-Complex Sentences – A compound-complex sentence has at least two independent clauses and at least one dependent clause.

   Examples:

   > John is my friend who went to India, and he brought souvenirs for us.
   > You may not know, but we heard the music that you played last night.

Review Video: Sentence Structure
Visit mometrix.com/academy and enter code: 700478

SENTENCE FRAGMENTS

A part of a sentence should not be treated like a complete sentence. A sentence must be made of at least one independent clause. An independent clause has a subject and a verb. Remember that the independent clause can stand alone as a sentence. Some fragments are independent clauses that begin with a subordinating word (e.g., as, because, so, etc.). Other fragments may not have a subject, a verb, or both.

A sentence fragment can be repaired in several ways. One way is to put the fragment with a neighbor sentence. Another way is to be sure that punctuation is not needed. You can also turn the fragment into a sentence by adding any missing pieces. Sentence fragments are allowed for writers who want to show off their art. However, for your exam, sentence fragments are not allowed.

Fragment: Because he wanted to sail for Rome.

Correct: He dreamed of Europe because he wanted to sail for Rome.

RUN-ON SENTENCES

Run-on sentences are independent clauses that have not been joined by a conjunction. When two or more independent clauses appear in one sentence, they must be joined in one of these ways:

1. Correction with a comma and a coordinating conjunction.
   Incorrect: I went on the trip and I had a good time.
   Correct: I went on the trip, and I had a good time.
2. Correction with a semicolon, a colon, or a dash. Used when independent clauses are closely related and their connection is clear without a coordinating conjunction.
   Incorrect: I went to the store and I bought some eggs.
   Correct: I went to the store; I bought some eggs.
3. Correction by separating sentences. This correction may be used when both independent clauses are long. Also, this can be used when one sentence is a question and one is not.
   Incorrect: The drive to New York takes ten hours it makes me very tired.
   Correct: The drive to New York takes ten hours. So, I become very tired.
4. Correction by changing parts of the sentence. One way is to turn one of the independent clauses into a phrase or subordinate clause.
   Incorrect: The drive to New York takes ten hours it makes me very tired.
   Correct: During the ten-hour drive to New York, I become very tired.

Note: Normally, one of these choices will be a clear correction to a run-on sentence. The fourth way can be the best correction but needs the most work.

> **Review Video: Fragments and Run-on Sentences**
> Visit mometrix.com/academy and enter code: 541989

DANGLING AND MISPLACED MODIFIERS
DANGLING MODIFIERS

A dangling modifier is a verbal phrase that does not have a clear connection to a word. A dangling modifier can also be a dependent clause (the subject and/or verb are not included) that does not have a clear connection to a word.

Examples:

77

Dangling: *Reading each magazine article*, the stories caught my attention.

Corrected: Reading each magazine article, *I* was entertained by the stories.

In this example, the word *stories* cannot be modified by *Reading each magazine article*. People can read, but stories cannot read. So, the pronoun *I* is needed for the modifying phrase *Reading each magazine article*.

Dangling: Since childhood, my grandparents have visited me for Christmas.

Corrected: Since childhood, I have been visited by my grandparents for Christmas.

In this example, the dependent adverb clause *Since childhood* cannot modify grandparents. So, the pronoun *I* is needed for the modifying adverb clause.

MISPLACED MODIFIERS

In some sentences, a modifier can be put in more than one place. However, you need to be sure that there is no confusion about which word is being explained or given more detail.

Incorrect: He read the book to a crowd that was filled with beautiful pictures.

Correct: He read the book that was filled with beautiful pictures to a crowd.

The crowd is not filled with pictures. The book is filled with pictures.

Incorrect: John only ate fruits and vegetables for two weeks.

Correct: John ate *only* fruits and vegetables for two weeks.

John may have done nothing else for two weeks but eat fruits and vegetables and sleep. However, it is reasonable to think that John had fruits and vegetables for his meals. Then, he continued to work on other things.

SPLIT INFINITIVES

A split infinitive occurs when a modifying word comes between the word *to* and the verb that pairs with *to*.

Example: To *clearly* explain vs. *To explain* clearly | To *softly* sing vs. *To sing* softly

Though still considered improper by some, split infinitives may provide better clarity and simplicity than the alternatives. As such, avoiding them should not be considered a universal rule.

DOUBLE NEGATIVES

Standard English allows two negatives when a positive meaning is intended. For example, "The team was not displeased with their performance." Double negatives that are used to emphasize negation are not part of Standard English.

Negative modifiers (e.g., never, no, and not) should not be paired with other negative modifiers or negative words (e.g., none, nobody, nothing, or neither). The modifiers *hardly, barely*, and *scarcely* are also considered negatives in Standard English. So, they should not be used with other negatives.

PARALLELISM AND SUBORDINATION

PARALLELISM

Parallel structures are used in sentences to highlight similar ideas and to connect sentences that give similar information. Parallelism pairs parts of speech, phrases, or clauses together with a matching piece. To write, *I enjoy <u>reading</u> and <u>to study</u>* would be incorrect. An infinitive does not match with a gerund. Instead, you should write *I enjoy <u>reading</u> and <u>studying</u>*.

Be sure that you continue to use certain words (e.g., articles, linking verbs, prepositions, infinitive sign (to), and the introductory word for a dependent clause) in sentences.

Incorrect: Will you bring the paper and pen with you?

Correct: Will you bring *the* paper and *a* pen with you?

Incorrect: The animals can come to eat and play.

Correct: The animals can come *to* eat and *to* play.

Incorrect: You are the person who remembered my name and cared for me.

Correct: You are the person *who* remembered my name and *who* cared for me.

SUBORDINATION

When two items are not equal to each other, you can join them by making the more important piece an independent clause. The less important piece can become subordinate. To make the less important piece subordinate, you make it a phrase or a dependent clause. The piece of more importance should be the one that readers want or will need to remember.

Example:

(1) The team had a perfect regular season. (2) The team lost the championship.

Despite having a perfect regular season, *the team lost the championship.*

WORD USAGE

Word usage, or diction, refers to the use of words with meanings and forms that are appropriate for the context and structure of a sentence. A common error in word usage occurs when a word's meaning does not fit the context of the sentence.

Incorrect: Susie likes chips better then candy.

Correct: Susie likes chips better than candy.

Incorrect: The cat licked it's coat.

Correct: The cat licked its coat.

Review Video: <u>Word Usage</u>
Visit mometrix.com/academy and enter code: 197863

WORD CONFUSION

WHICH, THAT, AND WHO

Which is used for things only.

> Example: John's dog, *which was called Max,* is large and fierce.

That is used for people or things.

> Example: Is this the only book *that Louis L'Amour wrote?*

> Example: Is Louis L'Amour the author *that wrote Western novels?*

Who is used for people only.

> Example: Mozart was the composer *who wrote those operas.*

HOMOPHONES

Homophones are words that sound alike (or similar), but they have different **spellings** and **definitions**.

TO, TOO, AND TWO

To can be an adverb or a preposition for showing direction, purpose, and relationship. See your dictionary for the many other ways use *to* in a sentence.

> Examples: I went to the store. | I want to go with you.

Too is an adverb that means *also, as well, very, or more than enough.*

> Examples: I can walk a mile too. | You have eaten too much.

Two is the second number in the series of numbers (e.g., one (1), two, (2), three (3)...)

> Example: You have two minutes left.

THERE, THEIR, AND THEY'RE

There can be an adjective, adverb, or pronoun. Often, *there* is used to show a place or to start a sentence.

> Examples: I went there yesterday. | There is something in his pocket.

Their is a pronoun that is used to show ownership.

> Examples: He is their father. | This is their fourth apology this week.

They're is a contraction of *they are.*

> Example: Did you know that they're in town?

KNEW AND NEW

Knew is the past tense of *know*.

> Example: I knew the answer.

New is an adjective that means something is current, has not been used, or modern.

> Example: This is my new phone.

THEN AND THAN

Then is an adverb that indicates sequence or order:

> Example: I'm going to run to the library and then come home.

Than is special-purpose word used only for comparisons:

> Example: Susie likes chips better than candy.

ITS AND IT'S

Its is a pronoun that shows ownership.

> Example: The guitar is in its case.

It's is a contraction of *it is*.

> Example: It's an honor and a privilege to meet you.

Note: The *h* in honor is silent, so the sound of the vowel *o* must have the article *an*.

YOUR AND YOU'RE

Your is a pronoun that shows ownership.

> Example: This is your moment to shine.

You're is a contraction of *you are*.

> Example: Yes, you're correct.

AFFECT AND EFFECT

There are two main reasons that **affect** and **effect** are so often confused: 1) both words can be used as either a noun or a verb, and 2) unlike most homophones, their usage and meanings are closely related to each other. Here is a quick rundown of the four usage options:

Affect (n): feeling, emotion, or mood that is displayed

> Example: The patient had a flat *affect*. (i.e., his face showed little or no emotion)

Affect (v): to alter, to change, to influence

> Example: The sunshine *affects* the plant's growth.

Effect (n): a result, a consequence

> Example: What *effect* will this weather have on our schedule?

Effect (v): to bring about, to cause to be

> Example: These new rules will *effect* order in the office.

The noun form of *affect* is rarely used outside of technical medical descriptions, so if a noun form is needed on the test, you can safely select *effect*. The verb form of *effect* is not as rare as the noun form of *affect*, but it's still not all that likely to show up on your test. If you need a verb and you can't decide which to use based on the definitions, choosing *affect* is your best bet.

HOMOGRAPHS

Homographs are words that share the same spelling, and they have multiple meanings. To figure out which meaning is being used, you should be looking for context clues. The context clues give hints to the meaning of the word. For example, the word *spot* has many meanings. It can mean "a place" or "a stain or blot." In the sentence "After my lunch, I saw a spot on my shirt," the word *spot* means "a stain or blot." The context clues of "After my lunch..." and "on my shirt" guide you to this decision.

BANK

> (noun): an establishment where money is held for savings or lending

> (verb): to collect or pile up

CONTENT

> (noun): the topics that will be addressed within a book

> (adjective): pleased or satisfied

FINE

> (noun): an amount of money that acts a penalty for an offense

> (adjective): very small or thin

INCENSE

> (noun): a material that is burned in religious settings and makes a pleasant aroma

> (verb): to frustrate or anger

LEAD

> (noun): the first or highest position

> (verb): to direct a person or group of followers

OBJECT

> (noun): a lifeless item that can be held and observed

> (verb): to disagree

PRODUCE

> (noun): fruits and vegetables

> (verb): to make or create something

REFUSE

(noun): garbage or debris that has been thrown away

(verb): to not allow

SUBJECT

(noun): an area of study

(verb): to force or subdue

TEAR

(noun): a fluid secreted by the eyes

(verb): to separate or pull apart

Essay Structure

INTRODUCTION

An introduction announces the main point of the passage. Normally, the introduction ranges from 50 to 70 words (i.e., 3 or 4 sentences). The purpose of the introduction is to gain the reader's attention and conclude with the essay's main point. An introduction can begin with an interesting quote, question, or strong opinion that grabs the reader's attention. Your introduction should include a restatement of the prompt, a summary of the main points of your essay, and your position on the prompt (i.e., the thesis sentence/statement). Depending on the amount of available time, you may want to give more or less information on the main points of your essay. The important thing is to impress the audience with your thesis statement (i.e., your reason for writing the essay).

THESIS STATEMENT

A thesis gives the main idea of the essay. A temporary thesis should be established early in the writing process because it will serve to keep the writer focused as ideas develop. This temporary thesis is subject to change as you continue to write.

The temporary thesis has two parts: a topic (i.e., the focus of your paper based on the prompt) and a comment. The comment makes an important point about the topic. A temporary thesis should be interesting and specific. Also, you need to limit the topic to a manageable scope. These three criteria are useful tools to measure the effectiveness of any temporary thesis:

1. Does the focus of my essay have enough interest to hold an audience?
2. Is the focus of my essay specific enough to generate interest?
3. Is the focus of my essay manageable for the time limit? Too broad? Too narrow?

The thesis should be a generalization rather than a fact because the thesis prepares readers for facts and details that support the thesis. The process of bringing the thesis into sharp focus may help in outlining major sections of the work. Once the thesis and introduction are complete, you can address the body of the work.

> **Review Video: Thesis Statements**
> Visit mometrix.com/academy and enter code: 691033

SUPPORTING THE THESIS

Throughout your essay, the thesis should be explained clearly and supported adequately by additional arguments. The thesis sentence needs to contain a clear statement of the purpose of your essay and a comment about the thesis. With the thesis statement, you have an opportunity to state what is noteworthy of this particular treatment of the prompt. Each sentence and paragraph should build on and support the thesis.

When you respond to the prompt, use parts of the passage to support your argument or defend your position. With supporting evidence from the passage, you strengthen your argument because readers can see your attention to the entire passage and your response to the details and facts within the passage. You can use facts, details, statistics, and direct quotations from the passage to uphold your position. Be sure to point out which information comes from the original passage and base your argument around that evidence.

PARAGRAPHS

Following the introduction, you will begin with body paragraphs. A paragraph should be unified around a main point. Normally, a good topic sentence summarizes the paragraph's main point. A topic sentence is a general sentence that gives an introduction to the paragraph. The sentences that follow are a support to the topic sentence. You may use the topic sentence as the final sentence to the paragraph if the earlier sentences give a clear explanation of the topic sentence. Overall, you need to stay true to the main point. This means that you need to remove unnecessary sentences that do not advance the main point.

The main point of a paragraph requires adequate development (i.e., a substantial paragraph that covers the main point). A paragraph of two or three sentences does not cover a main point. This is true when the main point of the paragraph gives strong support to the argument of the thesis. An occasional short paragraph is fine as a transitional device. However, you should aim to have six to seven sentences for each paragraph.

METHODS OF DEVELOPING PARAGRAPHS

A common method of development in your essay can be done with **examples**. These examples are the supporting details to the main idea of a paragraph or passage. When you write about something that your audience may not understand, you can provide an example to show your point. When you write about something that is not easily accepted, you can give examples to prove your point.

Illustrations are extended examples that require several sentences. Well selected illustrations can be a great way to develop a point that may not be familiar to your audience. With a time limit, you may have enough time to use one illustration. So, be sure that you use one that connects well with your main argument.

Analogies make comparisons between items that appear to have nothing in common. Analogies are employed by writers to provoke fresh thoughts about a subject. They may be used to explain the unfamiliar, to clarify an abstract point, or to argue a point. Although analogies are effective literary devices, they should be used carefully in arguments. Two things may be alike in some respects but completely different in others.

Cause and effect is an excellent device used when the cause and effect are accepted as true. One way of using cause and effect is to state the effect in the topic sentence of a paragraph and add the causes in the body of the paragraph. With this method, your paragraphs can have structure which always strengthens writing.

TYPES OF PARAGRAPHS

A **paragraph of narration** tells a story or a part of a story. Normally, the sentences are arranged in chronological order (i.e., the order that the events happened). However, you can include flashbacks (i.e., beginning the story at an earlier time).

A **descriptive paragraph** makes a verbal portrait of a person, place, or thing. When you use specific details that appeal to one or more of the senses (i.e., sight, sound, smell, taste, and touch), you give your readers a sense of being present in the moment.

A **process paragraph** is related to time order (i.e., First, you open the bottle. Second, you pour the liquid, etc.). Usually, this describes a process or teaches readers how to perform a process.

Comparing two things draws attention to their similarities and indicates a number of differences. When you contrast, you focus only on differences. Both comparisons and contrasts may be used point-by-point or in following paragraphs.

Reasons for starting a new paragraph include:

1. To mark off the introduction and concluding paragraphs
2. To signal a shift to a new idea or topic
3. To indicate an important shift in time or place
4. To explain a point in additional detail
5. To highlight a comparison, contrast, or cause and effect relationship

CONCLUSION

A good conclusion should leave readers satisfied and provide a sense of completeness. Many conclusions state the thesis in different words and give a summary of the ideas in the body paragraphs. Some writers find ways to conclude in a dramatic fashion. They may conclude with a vivid image or a warning and remind readers of the main point. The conclusion can be a few sentences because the body of the text has made the case for the thesis. A conclusion can summarize the main points and offer advice or ask a question. You should never introduce new ideas or arguments in a conclusion. Also, you need to avoid vague and aimless endings. Instead, close with a clear and specific paragraph.

Argumentative and Persuasive Writing

Argumentative and persuasive writing takes a stand on a debatable issue, seeks to explore all sides of the issue, and finds the best possible solution. Argumentative and persuasive writing should not be combative or abusive. The word *argument* may remind you of two or more people shouting at each other and walking away in anger. However, an argumentative or persuasive essay should be a calm and reasonable presentation on your ideas for others to consider. When you write reasonable arguments, your goal is not to win or have the last word. Instead, you want to reveal current understanding of the question and suggest a solution to a problem. The purpose of argument and persuasion in a free society is to reach the best solution.

INTRODUCTION

The introduction of an essay that argues for or against an issue should end with a thesis sentence that gives a position (i.e., the side that you want to defend or oppose) on the prompt. The thesis should be supported by strong arguments that back up your position. The main points of your argument should have a growing effect which convinces readers that the thesis has merit. In your introduction, you should list the main points of your argument which will outline the entire argumentative essay.

SUPPORTING EVIDENCE

Evidence needs to be provided that supports the thesis and additional arguments. Most arguments must be supported by facts or statistics. Facts are something that is known with certainty and have been verified by several independent individuals. Examples and illustrations add an emotional component to arguments. With this component, you persuade readers in ways that facts and statistics cannot. The emotional component is effective when used with objective information that can be confirmed.

COUNTER ARGUMENTS

When you show both sides to the argument, you build trust with readers. The graders of your essay will be undecided or neutral. If you present only your side to the argument, your readers will be concerned at best. Showing the other side of the argument can take place anywhere in the essay, but one of the best places is after the thesis statement.

Building common ground with neutral or opposed readers can be appealing to skeptical readers. Sharing values with undecided readers can allow people to switch positions without giving up what they feel is important. For people who may oppose a position, they need to feel that they can change their minds without betraying who they are as a person. This appeal to having an open-mind can be a powerful tool in arguing a position without antagonizing other views. Objections can be countered on a point-by-point basis or in a summary paragraph. Be careful in how you point out flaws in counter arguments. If you are unfair to the other side of the argument, then you can lose trust with your audience.

Clearness in Writing

COHERENCE

A smooth flow of sentences and paragraphs without gaps or shifts is what is meant by coherent writing. When your writing is coherent, you give information in a way that helps your readers understand the connection between sentences or paragraphs. The ties between old and new information can be completed by several strategies.

TIPS FOR COHERENT WRITING

Linking ideas clearly from the topic sentence to the body of the paragraph is essential for a smooth transition. The topic sentence states the main point, and this should be followed by specific details, examples, and illustrations that support the topic sentence.

The **repetition of key words** adds coherence to a paragraph. You can avoid overuse of a keyword by using synonyms of the key word.

Changing verb tenses in a paragraph can be confusing for your readers. Try to minimize shifting sentences from one verb tense to another. These shifts affect the smooth flows of words and can disrupt the coherence of the paragraph.

TRANSITIONS

Transitions are bridges between what has been read and what is about to be read. Transitions smooth the reader's path between sentences and inform readers of connections to new ideas in the essay. When you think about the appropriate phrase for a transition, you need to consider the previous and upcoming sentences or paragraphs. Thus, transitional phrases should be used with care. Tone should be considered when you want to use a transitional phrase. For example, *in summary* would be preferable to the informal *in short*. Consider these transitions:

Restatement: He wanted to walk the trails at the park, *namely* Yosemite National Park.

Contrast: This could be the best option. *On the other hand*, this option may lead to more damage.

> **Review Video: Transitions in Writing**
> Visit mometrix.com/academy and enter code: 233246

AVOID UNCLEAR WORDS AND PHRASES

CLICHÉS

Clichés are phrases that have been overused to the point that the phrase has no importance or has lost the original meaning. The phrases have no originality and add very little to your writing. Therefore, you should try to avoid the use of clichés. The best revision for clichés is to delete them. If this does not seem possible, then a cliché can be changed so that it is not predictable and empty of meaning.

Examples:

When life gives you lemons, make lemonade.

Every cloud has a silver lining.

EUPHEMISMS

Euphemisms are acceptable words which replace language that seems too harsh or ugly. Normally, people use a euphemism when they speak about subjects such as death and bodily functions.

Examples:

My grandmother *passed away* this weekend.

He had to go to the *mens' room*.

These acceptable words can be unclear or misunderstood. If you are trying to decide between using a euphemism or avoiding a euphemism, then you should choose to avoid talking about the subject altogether. You want the graders of your work to understand your entire essay.

JARGON

Jargon is a specialized vocabulary that is used among members of a trade or profession. Since jargon is understood by a small audience, you should not use such vocabulary in your essay. Jargon includes exaggerated language that tries to impress rather than inform. Sentences filled with jargon are not precise and difficult to understand.

Examples:

"He is going to *toenail* these frames for us." (Toenail is construction jargon for nailing at an angle.)

"They brought in a *kip* of material today." (Kip refers to 1000 pounds in architecture and engineering.)

SLANG

Slang is an informal and sometimes private language that is understood by some individuals. Slang has some usefulness, but the language can have a small audience. Again, you should avoid this in your writing. While the grader of your exam may be aware of the word, he or she may not understand the use of the word as you do.

Examples:

"Yes, the event was a blast!" (In this sentence, *blast* means that the event was a great experience.)

"That attempt was an epic fail." (By *epic fail*, the speaker means that his or her attempt was not a success.)

Reviewing the Essay

REVISIONS

A writer's choice of words is a signature of their style. Careful thought about the use of words can improve a piece of writing. When you pay attention to the use of specific nouns rather than general ones, you can make your essay an exciting piece to read.

Example:

General: His kindness will never be forgotten.

Specific: His thoughtful gifts and bear hugs will never be forgotten.

Think about the kind of verbs that you use in your sentences. Active verbs (e.g., run, swim) should be about an action. Whenever possible, trade a linking verb for an active verb to provide clear examples for your arguments and to strengthen your essay overall.

Example:

Passive: The winners were called to the stage by the judges.

Active: The judges called the winners to the stage.

Revising sentences is done to make writing more effective. Editing sentences is done to correct any errors. Sentences are the building blocks of writing, and they can be changed by paying attention to sentence length, sentence structure, and sentence openings. You should add variety to sentence length, structure, and openings so that the essay does not seem boring or repetitive. A careful analysis of a piece of writing will expose these stylistic problems, and they can be corrected before you finish your essay. Changing up your sentence structure and sentence length can make your essay more inviting and appealing to readers.

RECURSIVE WRITING PROCESS

However you approach the essay, you may find comfort in knowing that the revision process can occur in any order. The recursive writing process is not as difficult as the phrase appears to you. Simply put, the recursive writing process means that the steps in the writing process occur in no particular order. For example, planning, drafting, and revising (all a part of the writing process) take place at about the same time and you may not notice that all three happen so close together. Truly, the writing process is a series of moving back and forth between planning, drafting, and revising. Then, more planning, more drafting, and more revising until your essay is complete.

> **Review Video: Recursive Writing Process**
> Visit mometrix.com/academy and enter code: 951611

EVALUATING THE DRAFT

If there is available time and you have finished your essay, then you should do an evaluation of your work. In a classroom setting, you would want to review all of your work (i.e., from brainstorming for ideas to your final draft) with a critical eye. However, with a limited amount of time in your exam, you will want to do a quick review of your essay. There is no single checklist that guarantees a complete and effective evaluation, but there are some things that can be considered:

1. Purpose - Does the draft accomplish everything that was contained in the prompt? Is the material and tone appropriate for the intended audience?
2. Focus - Does the introduction and the conclusion focus on the main point? Are all supporting arguments focused on the thesis?
3. Organization and Paragraphing - Are there enough transitions and appropriate paragraph breaks to guide the reader? Are any paragraphs too long or too short?
4. Content - Is the supporting material persuasive? Are all ideas fully developed? Is there any material that needs to be removed?
5. Point of view - Is the draft free of distracting shifts in point of view? Is the point of view appropriate for the subject and intended audience?

When you evaluate your draft, you can consider your essay as a grader of your exam would look over your essay. The changes that you make can improve the material in an important way. So, if you have the time for a review of your work, take advantage of it and make the necessary changes.

Practice Test Questions

Mathematics

1. If *y* = 2, what is the value of the following expression?

$$(y^9 / y^3) \times 2$$

    A. 128
    B. 16
    C. 8192
    D. 1008

2. Simplify the following:

$$\frac{16x^3 - 32x^2 + 8x}{4x}$$

    A. $4x^3 - 8x^2 + 2x$
    B. $12x^2 - 28x^2 + 4$
    C. $4x^2 - 8x + 2$
    D. $4x^2 + 8x + 2$

3. $x^2 + 8x + 16 = 0$

    Solve for *x*.

    A. $x = -4, 4$
    B. $x = 4$
    C. $x = -4$
    D. $x = -2, 2$

4. Use factoring to simplify the following:

$$x^2 + 7x + 12$$

    A. $(x + 6)(x + 2)$
    B. $(x + 4)(x + 3)$
    C. $(x + 6)(x + 1)$
    D. $(x + 5)(x + 2)$

5. If *a* = -6 and *b* = 7, then 4a(3b+5)+2b=?

    A. 638
    B. -485
    C. 850
    D. -610

6. Given a line with slope $m = -2$ that passes through the point (-3, 4), find the equation of the line in standard form.

    A. $2x + y - 2 = 0$
    B. $2x - y - 2 = 0$
    C. $2x + y + 2 = 0$
    D. $y = 2x + 2$

7. A line passes through points A (-3, 18) and B (5, 2). What is the slope of the line?

    A. 2
    B. -2
    C. 1/2
    D. -1/2

8. Which of the following numerals is not a prime number?

    A. 3
    B. 6
    C. 17
    D. 41

9. Which of the following is equal to the difference between 4^3 and 3^4?

    A. 0
    B. 1
    C. 27
    D. 17

10. What is the midpoint of points A (-20, 8) and B (5, 3)?

    A. (5.5, 7.5)
    B. (7.5, 5.5)
    C. (5.5, -7.5)
    D. (-7.5, 5.5)

11. Evaluate the following expression, if $x = 3$.

    $x^5 x^2 + y^0 =$

    A. 59,049
    B. 59,050
    C. 2,187
    D. 2,188

12. $9x - 3y + 8xy - 3$

If $x = 10$ and $y = -2$, what is the value of this expression?

    A. -67
    B. -61
    C. -79
    D. 241

13. Simplify the following: $9x (3x^2 + 2x - 9)$

    A. $27x^2 + 18x - 81$
    B. $27x^3 + 18x^2 - 81x$
    C. $12x^3 + 11x^2 - x$
    D. $27x^3 + 18x^2 - 18x$

14. Expand the following expression: $(2x - 5) (x + 7)$

    A. $2x^2 + 9x - 35$
    B. $11x - 35$
    C. $2x^2 - 19x - 35$
    D. $2x^2 + 9x + 35$

15. What is the value of $2x^2 + 5x - y^2$ when $x = 3$ and $y = 5$?

    A. -4
    B. 8
    C. 16
    D. 72

16. $(y^2 + 9y - 2) + (4y^2 - y - 5) =$

    A. $5y^2 + 8y - 7$
    B. $5y^2 + 8y + 10$
    C. $5y^2 + 10y - 7$
    D. $5y^2 + 10y + 10$

17. If $x^2 + 5x = 6$, then $x\ = ?$

    A. -6 or -1
    B. -6 or 1
    C. -1 or 6
    D. 1 or 6

18. What percent of 56 is 42?

    A. 60%
    B. 72.5%
    C. 75%
    D. 85%

19. What is 56% of 25?

    A. 10
    B. 11
    C. 12
    D. 14

20. Solve the following equation, $5(80 / 8) + (7 - 2) - (9 \times 5) =$

    A. -150
    B. 10
    C. 100
    D. 230

21. Solve the following equation $\dfrac{4 - (-12)}{-9 + 5} =$

    A. -8
    B. -4
    C. -2
    D. 4

22. If $x\ =\ 2y - 3$ and $2x\ +\frac{1}{2}\ y\ =\ 3$, then $y = ?$

    A. $-\dfrac{2}{3}$
    B. 1
    C. 2
    D. $\dfrac{18}{7}$

23. Solve for y using the following system of equations.

$$2x - 6y = 12$$
$$-6x + 14y = 42$$

    A. -19.5
    B. -52.5
    C. -2.44
    D. 6.56

24. If $6x + 2x - 26 = -5x$, then $\left[\frac{2x-1}{7}\right]^3 =$

    A. 0.08
    B. 0.19
    C. 1.29
    D. 12.7

25. If, $3(x + 14) = 4(x + 9)$, what does x equal?

    A. $x = 4$
    B. $x = 6$
    C. $x = 12$
    D. $x = 15$

26. Let $= \frac{x^4 - 2}{x^2 + 1}$. If x = -2, what is the value of y?

    A. $-3\frac{3}{5}$
    B. $2\frac{4}{5}$
    C. $-2\frac{4}{5}$
    D. $2\frac{2}{3}$

27. Which of the following expressions is a factor of the polynomial $x^2 - 4x - 21$?

    A. $(x - 4)$
    B. $(x - 3)$
    C. $(x + 7)$
    D. $(x - 7)$

28. What is the value of the y-intercept of the line described by the equation:

$$2x + 3y - 7 = 0 ?$$

    A. 7
    B. -7
    C. $\frac{7}{3}$
    D. $-\frac{7}{3}$

29. Which of the following is an expression equivalent to $\frac{a^8 b^{-9} c^2}{a^{-3} b^6 c^4}$?

   A. $\frac{a^5 c^2}{b^3}$

   B. $\frac{a^5}{b^3 c^2}$

   C. $\frac{a^5}{b^{15} c^2}$

   D. $\frac{a^{11}}{b^{15} c^2}$

30. Which of the following expressions is equivalent to $\sqrt[3]{8x^5 y^7}$?

   A. $8^3 x^{15} y^{21}$

   B. $8^3 x^{\frac{5}{3}} y^{\frac{21}{3}}$

   C. $2x^{15} y^{21}$

   D. $2x^{\frac{5}{3}} y^{\frac{7}{3}}$

Reading

Read each passage carefully. Since the assessment is not timed, take as much time as you need to read each passage. Each passage may have one or more questions.

A helpful strategy is to focus on the opening and ending sentences of each paragraph to identify the main idea. Another strategy is to look for key words or phrases within the passage that indicate the author's purpose or the meaning.

Reading Sample Questions:

Read the selection and answer the questions that follow.

Cultivation of Tomato Plants

Tomato plants should be started in window boxes or greenhouses in late March so that they will be ready for the garden after the last frost. Use a soil of equal parts of sand, peat moss and manure, and plant the seeds about a quarter of an inch deep. After covering, water them through a cloth to protect the soil and cover the box with a pane of glass. Keep the box in a warm place for a few days, then place it in a sunny window. After the second leaf makes its appearance on the seedling, transplant the plant to another box, placing the seedlings two inches apart. Another alternative is to put the sprouted seedlings in four-inch pots, setting them deeper in the soil than they stood in the seed bed. To make the stem stronger, pinch out the top bud when the seedlings are four or five inches in height.

Finally, place the plants in their permanent positions after they have grown to be twelve or fifteen inches high. When transplanting, parts of some of the longest leaves should be removed. Large plants may be set five or six inches deep.

The soil should be fertilized the previous season. Fresh, stable manure, used as fertilizer, would delay the time of fruiting. To improve the condition of the soil, work in a spade full of old manure to a depth of at least a foot. Nitrate of soda, applied at about two hundred pounds per acre, may be used to give the plant a good start.

Plants grown on supports may be set two feet apart in the row, with the rows three or four feet apart depending upon the variety. Plants not supported by stakes or other methods should be set four feet apart.

Unsupported vines give a lighter yield and much of the fruit is likely to rot during the wet seasons. Use well sharpened stakes about two inches in diameter and five feet long. Drive the stakes into the ground at least six inches from the plants so that the roots will not be injured. Tie the tomato vines to the stakes with strings made out of strips of cloth, as twine is likely to cut them. Care must be taken not to wrap the limbs so tightly as to interfere with their growth. The training should start before the plants begin to trail on the ground.

1. What is the overall purpose of this passage?
   A. To describe how soil should be treated in order to plant tomatoes.
   B. To give an overview of how tomato plants are cultured.
   C. To teach the reader how to operate a farm.
   D. To describe a method of supporting tomato vines.

2. What does the passage imply as the reason that the seeds not planted outdoors immediately?

    A. A late freeze might kill the seedlings.

    B. The soil outdoors is too heavy for new seedlings.

    C. A heavy rain might wash away the seedlings.

    D. New seedlings need to be close to one another and then be moved apart later.

3. What would happen if the bud weren't pinched out of the seedlings when they are in individual pots?

    A. The plants would be weaker.

    B. The plants would freeze.

    C. The plants would need more water.

    D. The plants would not survive as long.

4. Why is old manure preferred to fresh manure?

    A. Fresh manure delays the plant's production of tomatoes.

    B. Fresh manure smells worse.

    C. Old manure is less expensive.

    D. Old manure mixes more readily with nitrate of soda.

5. What is the purpose of the last paragraph?

    A. To explain why unsupported plants give rotten fruit.

    B. To explain why cloth is used rather than wire.

    C. To describe in detail how tomato plants are cultured.

    D. To instruct the reader in the method of supporting tomato vines for culture.

Read the selection and answer the questions that follow.

Garth

The next morning, she realized that she had slept. This surprised her – so long had sleep been denied her! She opened her eyes and saw the sun at the window. And then, beside it in the window, the deformed visage of Garth. Quickly, she shut her eyes again, feigning sleep. But he was not fooled. Presently she heard his voice, soft and kind: "Don't be afraid. I'm your friend. I came to watch you sleep, is all. There now, I am behind the wall. You can open your eyes."

The voice seemed pained and plaintive. The Hungarian opened her eyes, saw the window empty. Steeling herself, she arose, went to it, and looked out. She saw the man below, cowering by the wall, looking grief-stricken and resigned. Making an effort to overcome her revulsion, she spoke to him as kindly as she could.

"Come," she said, but Garth, seeing her lips move, thought she was sending him away. He rose and began to lumber off, his eyes lowered and filled with despair.

"Come!" she cried again, but he continued to move off. Then, she swept from the cell, ran to him and took his arm. Feeling her touch, Garth trembled uncontrollably. Feeling that she drew him toward her, he lifted his supplicating eye and his whole face lit up with joy.

She drew him into the garden, where she sat upon a wall, and for a while they sat and contemplated one another. The more the Hungarian looked at Garth, the more deformities she discovered. The twisted spine, the lone eye, the huge torso over the tiny legs. She couldn't comprehend how a creature so awkwardly constructed could exist. And yet, from the air of sadness and gentleness that pervaded his figure, she began to reconcile herself to it.

"Did you call me back?" asked he.

"Yes," she replied, nodding. He recognized the gesture.

"Ah," he exclaimed. "Do you know that I am deaf?"

"Poor fellow," exclaimed the Hungarian, with an expression of pity.

"You'd think nothing more could be wrong with me," Garth put in, somewhat bitterly. But he was happier than he could remember having been.

6. During this passage, how do the girl's emotions toward Garth change?
  A. They go from anger to fear.
  B. They go from hatred to disdain.
  C. They go from fear to disdain.
  D. They go from revulsion to pity.

7. What is a synonym for the word *supplicating*?
  A. Castigating
  B. Menacing
  C. Repeating
  D. Begging

8. Which of the following adjectives would you use to describe Garth's feelings toward himself?
  A. Contemplative
  B. Destitute
  C. Unhappy
  D. Deflated

9. What two characteristics are contrasted in Garth?
  A. Ugliness and gentleness
  B. Fear and merriment
  C. Distress and madness
  D. Happiness and sadness

10. Why was the girl surprised that she had slept?
  A. She seldom slept.
  B. It had been a long time since she had had the chance to sleep.
  C. She hadn't intended to go to sleep.
  D. Garth looked so frightening that she thought he would keep her awake.

Read the selection and answer the questions that follow.

Leaving

Even though Martin and Beth's steps were muffled by the falling snow, Beth could still hear the faint crunch of leaves underneath. The hushed woods had often made Beth feel safe and at peace, but these days they just made her feel lonely.

"I'm glad we decided to hike the trail, Martin. It's so quiet and pretty."

"Sure."

Beth couldn't understand how it happened, but over the past few months this silence had grown between them, weighing down their relationship. Of course, there was that thing with Mary, but Beth had forgiven Martin. They moved on. It was in the past.

"Do you want to see a movie tonight?" asked Beth. "There's a new one showing at the downtown theater."

"Whatever you want."

She wanted her husband back. She wanted the laughter and games. She wanted the late-night talks over coffee. She wanted to forget Mary and Martin together. She wanted to feel some sort of <u>rapport</u> again.

"Is everything alright, Martin?"

"I'm fine. Just tired."

"We didn't have to come; we could have stayed at home."

"It's fine."

Beth closed her eyes, tilted her head back, and breathed in the crisp air. "Fine" once meant "very good," or "precious." Now, it is a meaningless word, an excuse not to tell other people what's on your mind. "Fine" had hung in the air between them for months now, a softly falling word that hid them from each other. Beth wasn't even sure she knew Martin anymore, but she was confident that it was only a matter of time before everything was not "fine," only a matter of time before he told her…

"I have to leave."

"Huh? What?"

"I got a page. My patient is going into cardiac arrest."

"I wish you didn't have to leave."

"I'm sorry, but I have to go."

"I know."

100

11. **It is reasonable to infer that Martin and Beth's relationship is strained because:**
    A. Martin recently lost his job.
    B. Martin was unfaithful to Beth.
    C. Martin works too much.
    D. Martin does not want to go to the movies.

12. **According to Beth, the word "fine" means:**
    A. "good"
    B. "precious"
    C. "very good"
    D. Nothing—it is a meaningless word.

13. **The best definition of the underlined word *rapport* is:**
    A. a close relationship.
    B. a sense of well-being.
    C. a common goal.
    D. loneliness.

14. **Based on the passage, it is reasonable to infer that Martin is a:**
    A. mechanic.
    B. medical doctor.
    C. dentist.
    D. film director.

15. **Based on Beth's perception of her and Martin's relationship, it is reasonable to infer:**
    A. Martin is dissatisfied with his job.
    B. Beth wants to have a baby.
    C. Martin is going to leave Beth.
    D. Martin and Beth have not known each other long.

Read the selection and answer the questions that follow.

New Zealand Inhabitants

The islands of New Zealand are among the most remote of all the Pacific islands. New Zealand is an archipelago, with two large islands and a number of smaller ones. Its climate is far cooler than the rest of Polynesia. Nevertheless, according to Maori legends, it was colonized in the early fifteenth century by a wave of Polynesian voyagers who traveled southward in their canoes and settled on North Island. At this time, New Zealand was already known to the Polynesians, who had probably first landed there some 400 years earlier.

The Polynesian southward migration was limited by the availability of food. Traditional Polynesian tropical crops such as taro and yams will grow on North Island, but the climate of the South Island is too cold for them. Coconuts will not grow on either island. The first settlers were forced to rely on hunting and gathering, and, of course, fishing. Especially on the South Island, most settlements remained close to the sea. At the time of the Polynesian influx, enormous flocks of moa birds had their rookeries on the island shores. These flightless birds were easy prey for the settlers, and within a few centuries had been hunted to extinction. Fish, shellfish and the roots of the fern were other important sources of food, but even these began to diminish in quantity as the human population increased. The Maori had few other sources of meat: dogs, smaller birds, and rats. Archaeological evidence shows that human flesh was also eaten, and that tribal warfare increased markedly after the moa disappeared.

By far the most important farmed crop in prehistoric New Zealand was the sweet potato. This tuber is hearty enough to grow throughout the islands, and could be stored to provide food during the winter months, when other food-gathering activities were difficult. The availability of the sweet potato made possible a significant increase in the human population. Maori tribes often lived in encampments called *pa*, which were fortified with earthen embankments and usually located near the best sweet potato farmlands.

16. A definition for the word *archipelago* is

- A. A country
- B. A place in the southern hemisphere
- C. A group of islands
- D. A roosting place for birds

17. This article is primarily about what?

- A. The geology of New Zealand
- B. New Zealand's early history
- C. New Zealand's prehistory
- D. Food sources used by New Zealand's first colonists.

18. According to the passage, when was New Zealand first settled?

- A. In the fifteenth century
- B. Around the eleventh century
- C. Thousands of years ago
- D. By flightless birds

19. What was a significant difference between the sweet potato and other crops known to the Polynesians?

- A. The sweet potato provided more protein.
- B. The sweet potato would grow on North Island.
- C. The sweet potato could be stored during the winter.
- D. The sweet potato could be cultured near their encampments.

20. Why was it important that sweet potatoes could be stored?

- A. They could be eaten in winter, when other foods were scarce.
- B. They could be traded for fish and other goods.
- C. They could be taken along by groups of warriors going to war.
- D. They tasted better after a few weeks of storage.

21. What was it about the moa that made them easy for the Maori to catch?

- A. They were fat.
- B. They roosted by the shore.
- C. They were not very smart.
- D. They were unable to fly.

22. Why did early settlements remain close to the sea?

    A. The people liked to swim.
    B. The people didn't want to get far from the boats they had come in.
    C. Taro and yams grow only close to the beaches.
    D. They were dependent upon sea creatures for their food.

Read the selection and answer the questions that follow.

Daylight Saving Time

Daylight Saving Time (DST) is the practice of changing clocks so that afternoons have more daylight and mornings have less. Clocks are adjusted forward one hour in the spring and one hour backward in the fall. The main purpose of the change is to make better use of daylight.

DST began with the goal of conservation. Benjamin Franklin suggested it as a method of saving on candles. It was used during both World Wars to save energy for military needs. Although DST's potential to save energy was a primary reason behind its implementation, research into its effects on energy conservation are contradictory and unclear.

Beneficiaries of DST include all activities that can benefit from more sunlight after working hours, such as shopping and sports. A 1984 issue of Fortune magazine estimated that a seven-week extension of DST would yield an additional $30 million for 7-Eleven stores. Public safety may be increased by the use of DST: some research suggests that traffic fatalities may be reduced when there is additional afternoon sunlight.

On the other hand, DST complicates timekeeping and some computer systems. Tools with built-in time-keeping functions such as medical devices can be affected negatively. Agricultural and evening entertainment interests have historically opposed DST.

DST can affect health, both positively and negatively. It provides more afternoon sunlight in which to get exercise. It also impacts sunlight exposure; this is good for getting vitamin D, but bad in that it can increase skin cancer risk. DST may also disrupt sleep.

Today, daylight saving time has been adopted by more than one billion people in about 70 countries. DST is generally not observed in countries near the equator because sunrise times do not vary much there. Asia and Africa do not generally observe it. Some countries, such as Brazil, observe it only in some regions.

DST can lead to peculiar situations. One of these occurred in November, 2007 when a woman in North Carolina gave birth to one twin at 1:32 a.m. and, 34 minutes later, to the second twin. Because of DST and the time change at 2:00 a.m., the second twin was officially born at 1:06, 26 minutes earlier than her brother.

23. According to the passage, what is the main purpose of DST?
  A. To increase public safety
  B. To benefit retail businesses
  C. To make better use of daylight
  D. To promote good health

24. Which of the following is not mentioned in the passage as a negative effect of DST?
  A. Energy conservation
  B. Complications with time keeping
  C. Complications with computer systems
  D. Increased skin cancer risk

25. The article states that DST involves:
  A. Adjusting clocks forward one hour in the spring and the fall.
  B. Adjusting clocks backward one hour in the spring and the fall.
  C. Adjusting clocks forward in the fall and backward in the spring.
  D. Adjusting clocks forward in the spring and backward in the fall.

26. Which interests have historically opposed DST, according to the passage?
  A. retail businesses and sports
  B. evening entertainment and agriculture
  C. 7-Eleven and health
  D. medical devices and computing

27. According to the article, increased sunlight exposure:
  A. is only good for health.
  B. is only bad for health.
  C. has no effect on health.
  D. can be both good and bad for health.

28. What is an example given in the passage of a peculiar situation that DST has caused?
  A. sleep disruption
  B. driving confusion
  C. twin birth order complications
  D. countries with DST only in certain regions

29. For what purpose did Benjamin Franklin first suggest DST?
  A. to save money for military needs
  B. to save candles
  C. to reduce traffic fatalities
  D. to promote reading

30. In what region does the article state DST is observed only in some regions?
  A. The equator
  B. Asia
  C. Africa
  D. Brazil

Writing

Read the selection and answer the questions 1-5.

(1) I had the same teacher for both third and 4th grades, which were difficult years for me. (2) My teacher and I did not get along, and I don't think she liked me. (3) Every day, I thought she was treating me unfairly and being mean. (4) Because I felt that way, I think I acted out and stopped doing my work. (5) In the middle of fourth grade, my family moved to a new town, and I had Mr. Shanbourne as my new teacher.

(6) From the very first day in Mr. Shanbourne's class, I was on guard. (7) I was expecting to hate my teacher and for him to hate me back when I started his class. (8) Mr. Shanbourne took me by surprise right away when he asked me if I wanted to stand up and introduce myself. (9) I said no, probably in a surly voice, and he just nodded and began teaching the first lesson of the day.

(10) I wasn't sure how to take this. (11) My old teacher forced me to do things and gave me detention if I didn't. (12) She loved detention and gave it to me for anything I did--talking back, working too loudly, forgetting an assignment. (13) Mr. Shanbourne obviously didn't believe in detention, and I tried him! (14) During my first two weeks at my new school I did my best to get in trouble. (15) I zoned out in class, turned work in late, talked out in class, and handed in assignments after the due date. (16) Mr. Shanbourne just nodded.

(17) Mr. Shanbourne asked me to stay in during recess. (18) *This is it*, I thought. I was going to get in trouble, get the detention my ten-year-old self had practically been begging for. (19) After all of the other kids ran outside, I walked up to Mr. Shanbourne's desk.

(20) "How are you doing, Alberto," he said.

(21) I mumbled something.

(22) He told me he was disappointed in my behavior over the last two weeks. (23) I had expected this and just took it. (24) The detention was coming any second. (25) Than Mr. Shanbourne took me by surprise. (26) He told me that even though he didn't know me very well, he believed I could be a hard worker and that I could be successful in his class. (27) He asked me how he could help listen better and turn my work in on time.

(28) I told him I had to think about it and rushed out to recess. (29) Even though my answer seemed rude, I was stunned. (30) I hadn't had a teacher in years who seemed to care about me, and said he believed in my abilities.

(31) To be honest, my behavior did not improve right away and I still turned in many of my assignments late. (32) But over the last few months of fourth grade, things changed. (33) Mr. Shanbourne continued to believe in me, encuorage me and help me, and I responded by doing my best. (34) I had a different teacher for fifth grade, but whenever I was struggling I walked down to Mr. Shanbourne's classroom to get his advice. (35) I'll never forget how Mr. Shanbourne helped me, and I hope he'll never forget me either.

1. What change should be made to sentence 1?

    A. Change *teacher* to *teachers*

    B. Change *4th* to *fourth*

    C. Delete the comma after *grades*

    D. Change *years* to *year's*

2. What is the most effective way to revise sentence 7?

    A. I started his class expecting my teacher to hate me back and for me to hate him.

    B. Expecting to hate my teacher, I started his class expecting him to hate me back.

    C. Starting his class expecting to hate my teacher, I also expected to hate him back.

    D. I started his class expecting to hate my teacher and for him to hate me back.

3. What is the most effective way to combine sentences 10 and 11?

    A. I wasn't sure how to take this, and my old teacher forced me to do things and gave me detention if I didn't.

    B. I wasn't sure how to take this, although my old teacher forced me to do things and gave me detention if I didn't.

    C. I wasn't sure how to take this because my old teacher forced me to do things and gave me detention if I didn't.

    D. I wasn't sure how to take this as a result of my old teacher forced me to do things and gave me detention if I didn't.

4. Which phrase, if any, can be deleted from sentence 15 without changing the meaning of the sentence?

    A. zoned out in class

    B. talked out in class

    C. handed in assignments after the due date

    D. No change

5. What transition should be added to the beginning of sentence 16?

    A. Surprisingly

    B. Actually

    C. Furthermore

    D. Instead

6. Which of the following choices best completes the sentence?

When at last Amber was able to _____ the numerous difficulties associated with the task, she concluded the wisdom of her grandfather was not only desirable, but absolutely necessary.

    A. perceive

    B. perception

    C. perceptive

    D. perceived

7. Which of the following words best completes the sentence?

The plan seemed flawless until its execution. The flames from the modified grill licked the bottom portion of the new wooden deck. Emil's elation warped into horror as he began to sweat. His grandparents had been extremely angry with the experiment on their car and his grandfather's red face hung before his eyes like a dark vision: "Before you _____ some other wild plan, talk to me first so we don't need to bring in the fire department."

  A. concoct
  B. invent
  C. make
  D. design

8. Which of the following sentences shows the correct usage of the hyphen?

  A. Miriam was a real-estate-broker with Hendry and Henderson, so she understood the importance of a well-cared-for home.
  B. Felipe dialed Joyce's number since it was easy-to-remember and listened with baited breath.
  C. Although Biraju was not an accident-prone person, he knew his older brother did not share this trait.
  D. James and Henry, both twenty-one year old students, had been able to pass the difficult test for medical school.

9. Which of the following choices is misspelled?

  A. conciliatory
  B. paroxism
  C. malevolence
  D. pernicious

10. Which of the following word choices completes the sentence?

Matthew posted the notice in the main hall and then proceeded to pass out the rest of the invitations to the _____ until his backpack was empty.

  A. receive
  B. reception
  C. receivable
  D. receiving

11. Read the following topic sentence from an opinion piece. Which of the following choices could provide some support for the topic sentence?

"Expansionary monetary policies are not the best option during a recession."

  A. Increasing the money supply may serve temporarily to boost the economy, but such an action damages the value of the dollar in the long run.
  B. Basing fiscal decisions on government tax cuts is similar to deciding suddenly that one does not require additional income, and therefore no longer accepting dividend payments.
  C. Allowing the government to control an entire industry would fly in the face of the Founding Fathers, since it not only takes away liberties but also puts businesses in the hands of politicians.
  D. Decreasing the interest rates may be the only successful way to drive business to the banks, and encouraging small business long has been known to generate wealth.

12. Read the claim below. Which of the following supports a counterclaim?

"Schools need to provide year-round education for students. Since the evolution of our society has moved us from an agrarian population to a largely urban one, there is no longer any need for the two month break during the summer. It is, in fact, a waste of students'—and society's—precious time."

A. The prospect of a year-round education for students is akin to an endless prison sentence; however, the inmates in this case cannot speak for themselves. They are the most vulnerable among us, and there is no one who will be their voice in this debate. Let's face it. This debate isn't about longer school days to help children, it's about providing more funding to the school staff.

B. There's a reason teachers are fleeing the public school system. It's broken. Teachers often work long hours in difficult conditions—imagine having the occupant of your office throw a paper airplane at you while you are working—and get paid little. A longer school day punishes teachers who are already sweating blood over their occupation. Teachers not only work through the school day, but often spend hours at home, developing curricula, grading papers, and preparing for the following day.

C. The limitations of this view are clear: there are no scientifically-backed works establishing that students perform better if they spend more time in school. However, there is significant research establishing the idea that learners do require time for creative pursuits and thinking. This supports the necessity of a summer break. In fact, it may be necessary to provide longer semester breaks so children have more time for their own creative pursuits.

D. In the interests of fairness, we must consider the possibility of a longer school day.

13. Which choice best completes the sentences below?

Our energy needs are not being adequately met, and in only a few short decades, we will be unable to satisfy the growing demand _____, no one has developed a plan to address those needs. Both sides of the argument have facts, science, and history to back their claims _____, fossil fuels are widely-used and available. _____, there is a limited supply of them and they damage the environment.

  A. So it seems, Similar to other claims, However
  B. However, On one hand, On the other hand
  C. On one hand, However, Similarly
  D. Strangely, First of all, Second of all

14. Which of the following shows the correct punctuation for this quote from Richard Feynman?

  A. If you thought that science was certain—well, that is just an error on your part.
  B. If you thought that science was certain, well that is just an error on your part.
  C. If you thought that, science was certain, well, that is just an error—on your part.
  D. If you thought—that science was certain—well, that is just an error on your part.

15. Which of the following best completes the sentence?

_____ is a kind of reaction where a small molecule of something gets added into a carbon-carbon bond.

  A. oxidation
  B. reduction
  C. addition reaction
  D. addition polymerization

16. Which of the following words is NOT spelled correctly?

  A. complacency
  B. indissoluble
  C. indefategable
  D. voracious

17. Which of the following is essential in a concluding statement of an argument?

  A. The introduction of new points that might lead to future arguments.
  B. A summary of the issue that reinforces clearly its main points.
  C. A contradiction of the argument's main points to provide fresh perspectives.
  D. An unrelated detail that might lighten the audience's mood after a heated debate.

18. Read the sentences, and then answer the question that follows.

I often have heard arguments claiming that complete freedom of speech could lead to dangerous situations. Without complete freedom of speech, we hardly are living in a free society.

Which word would best link these sentences?

    A. However
    B. Therefore
    C. So
    D. Supposedly

19. Which of the following statements best would conclude an essay about playwright William Shakespeare?

    A. William Shakespeare died of unknown causes on April 23, 1616.
    B. William Shakespeare wrote the most important plays ever written, and I think his best one is definitely Romeo and Juliet.
    C. William Shakespeare's plays have been staged in theaters throughout the world, yet he will always be most closely associated with the Globe Theater in London.
    D. Although William Shakespeare died in 1616, the artistry and eternal relevance of his work destined it to thrive for hundreds of years into the future.

20. Read the sentences, and then answer the question that follows.

In the past, television has been criticized as a medium without the complexity and artfulness of cinema. Contemporary programs, such as "Mad Men," are widely celebrated for their intricately structured narratives and beautifully realized design.

Which of the following statements best links these sentences?

    A. Today's television shows prove that the medium has not changed much.
    B. "Mad Men" is a television show about the advertising business of the 1960s.
    C. This attitude has changed drastically over time.
    D. Television now offers a wide range of comedies, dramas, and reality shows.

21. Which version of the sentence is written correctly?

    A. A Los-Angeles-area homeowner decided to relocate to San Francisco.
    B. A Los Angeles area homeowner decided to relocate to San Francisco.
    C. A Los Angeles-area homeowner decided to relocate to San Francisco.
    D. A Los-Angeles-area-homeowner decided to relocate to San Francisco.

22. Which version of the sentence is written correctly?

    A. Please lie the porcelain vase down gently to avoid chipping it.
    B. Please lain the porcelain vase down gently to avoid chipping it.
    C. Please lies the porcelain vase down gently to avoid chipping it.
    D. Please lay the porcelain vase down gently to avoid chipping it.

23. As used in the sentence, "The beach is at its most placid at sunset, after most people have gone home," what does the word placid mean?

    A. peaceful
    B. pitiful
    C. pretty
    D. picturesque

24. Which version of the sentence does NOT contain any misspelled words?

A. The pompouse man thought he was better than everyone else.
B. The pompous man thought he was better than everyone else.
C. The pompus man thought he was better than everyone else.
D. The pompis man thought he was better than everyone else.

25. Which version of the sentence creates the best feeling of suspense?

A. The owl pounced on the rabbit suddenly when it spied the helpless animal emerging from the brush.
B. When the owl spied the rabbit emerging from the brush, it pounced on the helpless animal suddenly.
C. It pounced on the helpless animal suddenly when the owl spied the rabbit emerging from the brush.
D. Suddenly, the owl pounced on the rabbit when it spied the helpless animal emerging from the brush.

26. Which of the following choices is the best way to write the sentence?

A. There is no way to instantly learn a new language.
B. Instantly there is no way to learn a new language.
C. There is no instantly way to learn a new language.
D. There is no way to learn a new language instantly.

27. Which of the following choices best completes the passage?

Standardized tests are becoming more important every year, and _____ these tests may seem like an easy way for educators to evaluate many students at once, there are considerable drawbacks. _____, teachers frequently teach to the test, which may raise scores but lowers the quality of education. _____: a recent survey showing that students know little information that is not tested on a standardized exam.

A. while, for example, case in point
B. since, while, interestingly
C. although, consequently, moreover
D. because, on the other hand, yet

28. Which of the following choices best completes the passage?

Genetic engineering is not just a new way of approaching the same breeding methods used by farmers for centuries. _____, it is a completely new way of dealing with living things. _____ some scientists say that we are only working with what nature has given us, this is clearly not the case. We are not working with nature, we are creating it. We are making ourselves gods.

A. However, For example
B. On the contrary, While
C. Notably, Case in point
D. First, Second

111

29. Which of the following sentences best completes the selection?

The flu is a common disease that plagues millions of Americans every year. Symptoms include a runny nose, fever, coughing, and an overall feeling of achiness. While there is little that can be done once someone catches the flu, there is one important step most people fail to take to prevent themselves from getting it.

A. They don't wash their hands when they go to the bathroom.
B. They fail to do something that is vital to protecting their health.
C. They only wash their hands if someone is watching them.
D. They fail to wash their hands thoroughly and frequently.

30. Which of the following is correct?

A. Mary had said: "I believe in the rights of my fellow man."
B. Since Fred: Jerry: and Peter wanted to go, they drove the van.
C. The Constitution: it is one of the greatest documents of all time: it is vital to our freedom.
D. Scientists need to keep finding new sources of money to support their research.

Answers and Explanations

Mathematics

1. A: $(y^9 \div y^3) \times 2$

Since we know that $y = 2$, it is simply a matter of substituting this value into the equation.

$(2^9 \div 2^3) \times 2$

$(512 \div 8) \times 2$

$64 \times 2 = 128$

2. C: $\frac{16x^3 - 32x^2 + 8x}{4x}$

To simplify, each term in the numerator can be divided by $4x$ to eliminate the denominator. The law of exponents that indicates that $x^n/x^m = x^{n-m}$ must be observed.

We are left with: $4x^2 - 8x + 2$

3. C: $x^2 + 8x + 16 = 0$

To solve for x, simplify this equation through factoring.

$(x + 4)(x + 4) = 0$

$x + 4 = 0$

$x = -4$

4. B: $x^2 + 7x + 12$

This expression can be simplified by using factoring.

The factors are $(x + 4)(x + 3)$.

To check the answer, multiply the first, outside, inside, and last terms (FOIL).

$x^2 + 3x + 4x + 12$

Combine like terms.

$x^2 + 7x + 12$

5. D: First, compute the value enclosed by the parentheses, 3b+5= 3 x 7 + 5= 26. Next, compute 4a = -24. Note that a is negative, so that this product is negative as well. The product 4a(3b+5) will therefore be negative as well, and equals -624. Finally, add the value of 2b, or 2 x 7 =14, to -624, to get the final answer -624+14=610.

113

6. C: The point-slope form of an equation is $(y - y_1) = m(x - x_1)$ given slope m and a point (x_1, y_1). The problem gives the slope $m = -2$ and the point $(x_1, y_1) = (-3, 4)$. Substitute these values into the point-slope form:

$$(y - y_1) = m(x - x_1) \rightarrow (y - 4) = -2(x - (-3))$$

Distribute the -2 and combine like terms:

$$(y - 4) = -2(x - (-3)) \rightarrow y - 4 = -2(x + 3) \rightarrow y - 4 = -2x - 6 \rightarrow y = -2x - 2$$

Do not stop here. While this is a correct equation using the given parameters, it does not satisfy the requirements of the problem. You are told to find the equation in standard form, and you have slope-intercept form. Standard form is $ax + by + c = 0$. Rearrange the terms in your equation to fit this form:

$$y = -2x - 2 \rightarrow 2x + y + 2 = 0$$

7. B: To calculate the slope of a line, we simply have to figure out the change in y over the change in x.

$$\frac{18 - 2}{-3 - 5} = \frac{16}{-8} = -2$$

-2 is the slope of the line.

8. B: A: prime number has only two whole integer divisors, 1 and itself. This is true of 3, 17, and 41. However 6 can be divided by 1, 2, 3, and 6. It is therefore not a prime number.

9. D: Since $4^3 = 4 \times 4 \times 4 = 64$, and $3^4 = 3 \times 3 \times 3 \times 3 = 81$, the answer is $81 - 64 = 17$.

10. D: To find a midpoint, simply calculate the average of the two sets of points.

For x, the midpoint is calculated in the following manner:

(-20 + 5)/2 = -7.5

For y, the midpoint is calculated in the following manner:

(8 + 3)/2 = 5.5

The midpoint is (-7.5, 5.5)

11. D: $x^5 x^2 + y^0 =$

We know that $x = 3$.

Therefore, we can find the value of $x^5 x^2$

$3^5 3^2$

$243 \cdot 9 = 2{,}187$

We don't know the value of y, but any value to the power of zero is equal to one.

Therefore, $2{,}187 + 1 = 2{,}188$

12. A: Since we know the value of x and y, it is simply a matter of substituting them into the expression:

$9x - 3y + 8xy - 3$

$9(10) - 3(-2) + 8(10)(-2) - 3$

$90 + 6 - 160 - 3$

$96 - 163 = -67$

13. B: $9x(3x^2 + 2x - 9)$

To simplify, multiply the value outside of the brackets ($9x$) by the values inside of the brackets.

$9x \cdot 3x^2 + 9x \cdot 2x - 9x \cdot 9$

$27x^3 + 18x^2 - 81x$

14. A: $(2x - 5)(x+7)$

To expand, multiply the first terms, outside terms, inside terms, and then the last terms (FOIL)

$2x^2 + 14x - 5x - 35$

Combine like terms.

$2x^2 + 9x - 35$

15. B: To evaluate the expression for the given values of x and y, substitute the values into the expression and then calculate the result:

$2x^2 + 5x - y^2 = 2(3)^2 + 5(3) - (5)^2$

$= 2 \cdot 9 + 5 \cdot 3 - 25$

$$= 18 + 15 - 25$$

$$= 8$$

16. A: To add quadratic expressions, combine like terms. In this problem, there are three sets of like terms: the y^2-terms, the y-terms, and the constants. Set up the addition vertically, making sure to line up like terms, and then add them together:

$\quad y^2 + 9y - 2$

$\underline{+\ 4y^2 - y - 5}$

$\quad 5y^2 + 8y - 7$

17. B: The given equation is a quadratic equation that can be solved by factorization. First, move everything to one side to get it in the correct form, by subtracting 6 from both sides:

$$x^2 + 5x = 6$$

$$x^2 + 5x - 6 = 0$$

This factors out to:

$$(x + 6)(x - 1) = 0$$

Thus, the two solutions to the equation are $x = -6$ and $x = 1$.

18. C: A percent is a part divided by the whole $\left(\frac{\text{part}}{\text{whole}}\right)$. In this problem, the part is 42 and the whole is 56, so the ratio can be expressed as $\frac{42}{56}$, or 0.75:

$$\frac{42}{56} = 0.75 = 75\%$$

19. D: First convert the percent to a decimal number by dividing it by 100, or, equivalently, by moving the decimal point two places to the left:

$$56\% = 0.56$$

Next, calculate 56% of 25 by multiplying 25 by 0.56:

$$0.56 \times 25 = 14$$

20. B: 5 × (80 / 8) + (7 − 2) − (9 × 5) =

Remember the order of operations: Parentheses, exponents, multiplication, division, addition, subtraction.

Perform the operations inside the parentheses first:

5 × (10) + (5) − (45) =

Then, do any multiplication and division, working from left to right:

50 + 5 − 45 =

Finally, do any adding or subtracting, working from left to right:

55 − 45 = 10

21. B: According to the order of operations (PEMDAS), first simplify the numerator and the denominator of the expression, then perform the division:

$$\frac{4 - (-12)}{-9 + 5} = \frac{4 + 12}{-9 + 5} = \frac{16}{-4} = -4$$

22. C: The given equations form a system of linear equations. Since the first equation is already given in terms of x, it will be easier to solve it using the substitution method. Start by substituting $2y - 3$ for x in the second equation:

$$2x + \frac{1}{2}y = 3 \quad 2(2y - 3) + \frac{1}{2}y = 3$$

Next, solve the resulting equation for y. Distribute the 2 and then combine like y-terms in the result:

$$4y - 6 + \frac{1}{2}y = 3 \quad \frac{9}{2}y - 6 = 3$$

Finally, isolate the variable y by adding 6 to both sides and then dividing both sides by the coefficient of y, which is $\frac{9}{2}$ (or, equivalently, multiply by 2 and divide by 9):

$$\frac{9}{2}y = 9 \quad y = 2$$

23. A: $2x - 6y = 12$

$-6x + 14y = 42$

To solve a variable using a system of equations, one of the variables must be cancelled out. To eliminate x from these equations, first multiply the top equation by 3.

$3(2x - 6y = 12)$

$6x - 18y = 36$

Then, add the two equations to eliminate x.

$6x - 18y = 36$

$\underline{+\ -6x + 14y = 42}$

$-4y = 78$

Solve for y.

$-4y = 78$

$y = 78/-4$

$y = -19.5$

24. A: Use the first equation to solve for x.

$6x + 2x - 26 = -5x$

$8x + 5x = 26$

$13x = 26$

$x = 2$

Then, evaluate the second equation.

[(2*x* - 1)/7]³

[(2 × 2-1)/7]³

[3/7]³

[0.4285]³

= 0.0787

Rounding, we get 0.08

25. B: To solve, first do the multiplication on each side of the equation: $3x + 42 = 4x + 36$. Then get like terms on opposite sides of the equation: $x = 6$

26. B: The evaluation of the equation, for an x-value of –2, gives the following: $y = \frac{(-2)^4 - 2}{(-2)^2 + 1}$, which reduces to $y = \frac{16-2}{4+1}$, or $y = \frac{14}{5}$. The improper fraction, $\frac{14}{5}$, can also be written as the mixed number, $2\frac{4}{5}$. Thus, $y = 2\frac{4}{5}$.

27. D: The polynomial can be factored as $(x - 7)(x + 3)$. Thus, $(x - 7)$ is a factor of the given polynomial.

28. C: The linear equation can be rewritten as $y = -\frac{2}{3}x + \frac{7}{3}$. The slope-intercept form of an equation, or $y = mx + b$, includes m as the slope and b as the y-intercept. Therefore, the y-intercept of the equation is $\frac{7}{3}$.

29. D: When dividing terms with identical bases, the exponents are to be subtracted, i.e., $\frac{a^4}{a^3} = a^1$ or a. Thus, the rational expression can be rewritten $a^{11}b^{-15}c^{-2}$. The rules of exponents also state: $a^{-x} = \frac{1}{a^x}$. So, the rational expression can now be rewritten as $\frac{a^{11}}{b^{15}c^2}$.

30. D: The radical expression can be rewritten as the product, $\sqrt[3]{8x^3y^6}\sqrt[3]{x^2y}$, which simplifies to $2xy^2\sqrt[3]{x^2y}$. This product can be rewritten as $2xy^2(x^2y)^{\frac{1}{3}}$, or $2xy^2\left(x^{\frac{2}{3}}y^{\frac{1}{3}}\right)$. Multiplying the two expressions gives $2x^{\frac{5}{3}}y^{\frac{7}{3}}$.

Reading

1. B: The passage gives general instructions for tomato plant culture from seeding to providing support for the vines. Answers A and D are too specific, focusing on details of the text. Answer C is too general: the passage does not fully describe how to operate a farm.

2. A: The passage states that seeds germinated in late March will be ready for the garden after the last frost, implying that exposure to freezing temperatures would harm them.

3. A: The text states that pinching the bud is done to make the plants stronger.

4. A: The text states that use of fresh manure will delay fruiting.

5. D: Although all the other answers make mention of information contained in the paragraph, the overall purpose of this paragraph is as stated, to describe the support procedure.

6. D: At first repelled by the sight of Garth in the window, the girl eventually expresses pity when she learns that he is deaf, too.

7. D: When he lifted his supplicating eye, it was referring to the way that he was begging. He was giving her a begging look and then stopped.

8. C: Garth is sad that he is so deformed that other people are frequently repelled and try to avoid contact with him.

9. A: Despite his ugliness and deformity, Garth is a gentle soul who wants to be accepted as a friend by the girl.

10. B: In the first sentence the phrase "so long had sleep been denied her" tells us she had been prevented from sleeping for some time.

11. B: This question is concerned with the main idea of the passage. Although the passage is not explicit about why Martin and Beth's relationship is strained, by eliminating a number of answer choices, the right answer can easily be found. Choice A can be eliminated because Martin has not lost his job—he receives a page at the end of the passage concerning one of his patients. Choice B is not contradicted by the passage, but all that the reader is told is that Martin and Mary were once together. Choice C can be eliminated because the passage does not indicate how much Martin works. Choice D can be eliminated because Martin tells Beth that if she wants to go to the movies, they can go. The best choice, then, is B.

12. D: This question asks for the definition of "fine" within the passage. "Fine" can mean "good," "precious," or "sharp," but this question asks for the meaning of "fine" within the passage itself. Choices A and B are inappropriate because Beth says that "fine" used to mean these things but does not any longer. Choice C is inappropriate for the same reason: while "fine" can mean "very good" or "sharp," it does not mean these things within the passage. Choice D is the best answer because Beth says "fine" is "a meaningless word, an excuse not to tell other people what's on your mind." Even though "fine" can mean choices A–C, the question asks what "fine" means according to Beth. Thus, the best choice is D.

13. A: This question asks for the best definition of "rapport." A "rapport" is a relationship based on mutual understanding. With this in mind, Choice A might be a good answer, even though it is not an exact match. Choice B can be eliminated because it does not describe a relationship. Choice C can be eliminated because individuals can have a relationship based on mutual understanding without sharing a common goal. Choice D can be eliminated because loneliness or boredom have nothing to do with the definition of "rapport."

14. B: This question asks the reader to make a conclusion based on details from the passage. The reader knows that (1) Martin wears a pager for his job, (2) he has patients, and (3) one of his patients is going into cardiac arrest. Choices A and D can be eliminated because mechanics, film directors, and television producers do not see patients. Choice C seems like a possibility. After all, dentists see patients. Choice B is the best choice because if a person goes into cardiac arrest it is more likely a medical doctor rather than a dentist would be paged.

15. C: This question asks the reader to make an inference about what is going to happen based on the passage. Choice A is inappropriate because the passage says nothing about Martin's level of satisfaction with his job. Choice B is can be eliminated for a similar reason—the passage says nothing about Beth's desire for children. Choice C seems like a good choice because while Martin tells Beth he has to leave to go to work, the structure of the sentence immediately preceding this makes it seem as if Beth knows Martin is going to leave her: "Beth wasn't even sure she knew Martin anymore, but she was confident that it was only a matter of time before everything was not "fine," only a matter of time before he told her…" Choice D is inappropriate because there is nothing in the passage that indicates how long Beth and Martin have known each other. The best choice, then, is C.

16. C: An archipelago is a large group or chain of islands.

17. D: The article deals primarily with the ways the colonists fed themselves: their crops and the foods they hunted. While it also describes New Zealand's prehistory, the main focus is on food sources.

18. B: The article states that the islands were colonized by Polynesians in the fifteenth century but that the first settlers had arrived some 400 years earlier than that.

19. C: The sweet potato could be stored, providing a source of food during the winter when other food gathering activities were difficult.

20. A: The sweet potato provided a winter food source through storage, allowing the population to increase.

21. D: The moa were flightless birds, so they could not easily escape when the humans came to hunt them.

22. D: The passage states that the first settlers were forced to rely on fishing for their food.

23. C: The first paragraph states that the main purpose of DST it to make better use of daylight.

24. A: Energy conservation is discussed as a possible benefit of DST, not a negative effect of it.

25. D: The first paragraph states that DST involves setting clocks forward one hour in the spring and one hour backward in the fall.

26. B: The last sentence in paragraph four notes that agricultural and evening entertainment interests have historically been opposed to DST.

27. D: The passage gives examples of both good and bad effects extra daylight can have on health.

28. C: The last paragraph of the passage notes that DST can lead to peculiar situations, and relays an anecdote about the effect of DST on the birth order of twins.

29. B: In the second paragraph, the author asserts that Benjamin Franklin suggested DST as a way to save candles.

30. D: The sixth paragraph notes that DST is observed in only some regions of Brazil.

Writing

1. B: The word *fourth* should be written out to match the form of *third*. While the word *teacher* could become plural, choice A is incorrect because the second sentence of the passage shows that

Alberto is talking about a single teacher. Choice C is incorrect because the comma correctly separates two independent clauses. Choice D is incorrect because Alberto is talking about several years rather than the possessive of one year. Therefore, the form of *years* should be plural rather than possessive.

2. D: The correct answer is Choice D because it uses proper word order to get the point across. Choice D begins with a subject and verb and follows the verb by two objects. Choice A is incorrect because the phrases *my teacher to hate me back* and *for me to hate him* are written in reverse order. It is more logical for *for me to hate him* to be written first. Choice B is incorrect because the subject and verb separate Alberto's two emotions (*expecting to hate my teacher* and *expecting him to hate me back*). This separation makes the sentence more difficult to read and understand. Choice C is incorrect because Alberto states twice that he expected to hate Mr. Shanbourne.

3. C: The correct answer is Choice C because the word *because* combines the sentence by showing that the second clause is an explanation for the first clause. Choice A is incorrect because the conjunction *and* doesn't show how the two clauses are connected. Choice B is incorrect because the word *although* doesn't logically connect the two clauses. The word *although* implies that the two clauses contradict each other; instead, the second clause explains the first. Although *as a result of* has a similar meaning to *because* and could be used to effectively combine the sentences, choice D is incorrect because the verbs *forced* and *gave* should be changed to *forcing* and *giving* in order for *as a result of* to be used correctly.

4. C: The phrase *handed in assignments after the due date* is redundant with the phrase *turned in work late*; only one of those phrases needs to be in the sentence. Choices A and B are incorrect because both phrases add unique information to the sentence. Choice D is incorrect because the sentence has two redundant phrases, and one of them should be deleted.

5. A: The transition "surprisingly" indicates that the reaction was unexpected, or even contradictory to the circumstance of the speaker not turning his work in on time and talking-out in class. The other answer choices do not make as much sense to coordinate these two sentences.

6. A: perceive. This is the correct form of the word for the sentence.

7. A: concoct. While the words are all very similar in meaning (denotation), only *concoct* best matches the tone of the passage: Emil is prone to developing wild ideas that result in disaster. "Invent" (B) and "design" (D) have positive connotations, while "make" (C) has a neutral feeling about it.

8. C: Although Biraju was not an accident-prone person, he knew that his older brother did not share this trait. Only choice C correctly uses the hyphen. Hyphens are used for many reasons, such as to make an adjective and a noun a compound word or in numbers (fifty-seven). Choice A uses too many hyphens (real-estate-broker), B does not use "easy-to-remember" as an adjective, and D is missing hyphens "twenty-one-year-old students".

9. B: paroxysm. A paroxysm is a fit or sudden attack of a disease or emotion.

10. B: reception. The sentence clearly requires a noun. In this case, "reception" is the only word that correctly completes the sentence.

11. A: Increasing the money supply may serve temporarily to boost the economy, but such an action damages the value of the dollar in the long run. This is the only argument supporting the idea that printing money may not be the best option. Expansionary monetary policy refers to the government action of increasing the money supply. The other choices do not address this policy directly.

12. C: The limitations of this view are clear: there are no scientifically-backed works establishing that students perform better if they spend more time in school. However, there is significant research establishing the idea that learners do require time for creative pursuits and thinking. This supports the necessity of a summer break. In fact, it may be necessary to provide longer semester breaks so children have more time for their own creative pursuits. Only this choice develops and supports a counterclaim. Choice A provides a counterclaim but does not give support. Choice B does not address the claim. Choice D actually supports the claim, and adds on the issue of teacher salaries.

13. B: However, On one hand, On the other hand

This is the best choice because the first blank shows a change in the direction. The second blank is part of a sentence indicating that an initial point will be made. The final blank is in a sentence that indicates a contradiction has occurred.

14. A: If you thought that science was certain—well, that is just an error on your part.

This choice is the only one that is punctuated correctly. All of the other choices show incorrect ways of expressing the sentence.

15. C: addition reaction. This choice completes the sentence with the correct vocabulary. An addition reaction occurs when a smaller molecule is added into a double (or sometimes triple) carbon bond. Choice A is oxidation, which happens when a substance loses electrons. Choice B is reduction, which happens when a substance gains electrons, and Choice D refers to the joining of monomers.

16. C: indefategable. This word is spelled incorrectly; it should be "indefatigable." The other words are all correct.

17. B: The key to an effective concluding statement is a concise summary of the argument's main points. Such a conclusion leaves the opponent and audience with a clear and organized understanding of the argument. The introduction of new points or a detail merely added to lighten mood would weaken the argument by straying off point at the last minute. Introducing contradictory perspectives completely would work against the argument's effectiveness.

18. A: The first sentence introduces an argument against complete freedom of speech. The second sentence makes an argument in favor of it. The second sentence contradicts the first one, so the two sentences should be linked with the adverb "however." "Therefore" and "so" would be used only if the sentences supported each other.

19. D: This statement mentions the death of William Shakespeare, effectively indicating his end. It also refers to the importance of his work and the continued relevance of his work in the years to come, which is integral to any general essay about the playwright. This statement offers a stronger conclusion to an essay on William Shakespeare than stopping short with the cause and date of his death. In addition, this choice does not stray from an authoritative tone by presenting personal opinion about Shakespeare's best play or a random detail about the theaters that staged his work.

20. C: The first sentence explains how television once was criticized. The second sentence shows how contemporary shows now are being praised. They require a linking sentence indicating that an attitude change toward television has occurred over time. Explaining the premise of "Mad Men" or the variety of shows on television does not address the best way to link these sentences. Stating, "Today's television shows prove that the medium has not changed much," contradicts the second sentence.

21. C: A compound modifier consists of more than two words, which must be linked with one or more hyphen in order to be correct. In this sentence, "Los Angeles-homeowner" is a compound modifier. Although "Los Angeles" consists of two words, it is a single city name and does not require a hyphen between "Los" and "Angeles."

22. D: The words lie and lay often are confused, but they are not used in the same way. Lie means to recline, as a person might lie on a bed. Lay is a verb meaning to place an object. Since a porcelain vase is an object, the correct word is lay in this sentence.

23. A: Although the words pretty and picturesque make sense in the context of this sentence, it contains clues indicating a more accurate answer choice. When people leave an area, they take their noise and activities with them, leaving the place relatively peaceful. A beach would be at its most peaceful after people have left it after sunset. Based on this context, you can conclude that placid and peaceful have the same meaning.

24. B: The word pompous, meaning arrogant or self-important, is spelled with an "ou," creating an "uh" sound.

25. B: Although all of these sentences technically are correct, only choice B uses syntax to establish a feeling of suspense. It achieves this by saving the action—the owl pouncing on the rabbit—for the end of the sentence. The other answer choices give away the action right away.

26. D: Choices B and C clearly misuse the adverb "instantly" by placing it where it does not make sense. Choice A is more of a grey area. Placing "instantly" inside the phrase "to learn" creates a split infinitive. Technically, a split infinitive is a form of incorrect grammar, yet it has become so widely used that many people now accept it as correct. However, it remains technically incorrect, and choice D is the best answer choice.

27. A: while, for example, case in point

This is the best choice for this passage because an idea is introduced, and then there is a change in the direction. The change in direction acknowledges another point of view. The next sentence illustrates part of the author's argument with a supporting idea (standardized tests lower the quality of education). The last sentence is talking about a specific example and using the colon to break up the sentence.

28. B: On the contrary, while the transitions needed here must complete the sentences while preserving the direction of the passage. The first sentence gives us one direction, then the second sentence provides a contradiction. The third sentence is about what scientists are saying, but includes a contrasting comment.

29. D: They fail to wash their hands thoroughly and frequently.

This is the only choice that matches the style and tone of the passage. Choices A and C are too informal. Choice B does not complete the passage.

30. A: Mary had said: "I believe in the rights of my fellow man."

This is the only choice that uses the colon correctly; it introduces a quotation. The other choices do not use the colon in the correct way to introduce either a quotation or a list of items.How to Overcome Test Anxiety

Just the thought of taking a test is enough to make most people a little nervous. A test is an important event that can have a long-term impact on your future, so it's important to take it seriously and it's natural to feel anxious about performing well. But just because anxiety is normal, that doesn't mean that it's helpful in test taking, or that you should simply accept it as part of your life. Anxiety can have a variety of effects. These effects can be mild, like making you feel slightly nervous, or severe, like blocking your ability to focus or remember even a simple detail.

If you experience test anxiety—whether severe or mild—it's important to know how to beat it. To discover this, first you need to understand what causes test anxiety.

Causes of Test Anxiety

While we often think of anxiety as an uncontrollable emotional state, it can actually be caused by simple, practical things. One of the most common causes of test anxiety is that a person does not feel adequately prepared for their test. This feeling can be the result of many different issues such as poor study habits or lack of organization, but the most common culprit is time management. Starting to study too late, failing to organize your study time to cover all of the material, or being distracted while you study will mean that you're not well prepared for the test. This may lead to cramming the night before, which will cause you to be physically and mentally exhausted for the test. Poor time management also contributes to feelings of stress, fear, and hopelessness as you realize you are not well prepared but don't know what to do about it.

Other times, test anxiety is not related to your preparation for the test but comes from unresolved fear. This may be a past failure on a test, or poor performance on tests in general. It may come from comparing yourself to others who seem to be performing better or from the stress of living up to expectations. Anxiety may be driven by fears of the future—how failure on this test would affect your educational and career goals. These fears are often completely irrational, but they can still negatively impact your test performance.

Review Video: 3 Reasons You Have Test Anxiety
Visit mometrix.com/academy and enter code: 428468

Elements of Test Anxiety

As mentioned earlier, test anxiety is considered to be an emotional state, but it has physical and mental components as well. Sometimes you may not even realize that you are suffering from test anxiety until you notice the physical symptoms. These can include trembling hands, rapid heartbeat, sweating, nausea, and tense muscles. Extreme anxiety may lead to fainting or vomiting. Obviously, any of these symptoms can have a negative impact on testing. It is important to recognize them as soon as they begin to occur so that you can address the problem before it damages your performance.

> **Review Video: 3 Ways to Tell You Have Test Anxiety**
> Visit mometrix.com/academy and enter code: 927847

The mental components of test anxiety include trouble focusing and inability to remember learned information. During a test, your mind is on high alert, which can help you recall information and stay focused for an extended period of time. However, anxiety interferes with your mind's natural processes, causing you to blank out, even on the questions you know well. The strain of testing during anxiety makes it difficult to stay focused, especially on a test that may take several hours. Extreme anxiety can take a huge mental toll, making it difficult not only to recall test information but even to understand the test questions or pull your thoughts together.

> **Review Video: How Test Anxiety Affects Memory**
> Visit mometrix.com/academy and enter code: 609003

Effects of Test Anxiety

Test anxiety is like a disease—if left untreated, it will get progressively worse. Anxiety leads to poor performance, and this reinforces the feelings of fear and failure, which in turn lead to poor performances on subsequent tests. It can grow from a mild nervousness to a crippling condition. If allowed to progress, test anxiety can have a big impact on your schooling, and consequently on your future.

Test anxiety can spread to other parts of your life. Anxiety on tests can become anxiety in any stressful situation, and blanking on a test can turn into panicking in a job situation. But fortunately, you don't have to let anxiety rule your testing and determine your grades. There are a number of relatively simple steps you can take to move past anxiety and function normally on a test and in the rest of life.

> **Review Video: How Test Anxiety Impacts Your Grades**
> Visit mometrix.com/academy and enter code: 939819

Physical Steps for Beating Test Anxiety

While test anxiety is a serious problem, the good news is that it can be overcome. It doesn't have to control your ability to think and remember information. While it may take time, you can begin taking steps today to beat anxiety.

Just as your first hint that you may be struggling with anxiety comes from the physical symptoms, the first step to treating it is also physical. Rest is crucial for having a clear, strong mind. If you are tired, it is much easier to give in to anxiety. But if you establish good sleep habits, your body and mind will be ready to perform optimally, without the strain of exhaustion. Additionally, sleeping well helps you to retain information better, so you're more likely to recall the answers when you see the test questions.

Getting good sleep means more than going to bed on time. It's important to allow your brain time to relax. Take study breaks from time to time so it doesn't get overworked, and don't study right before bed. Take time to rest your mind before trying to rest your body, or you may find it difficult to fall asleep.

> **Review Video: <u>The Importance of Sleep for Your Brain</u>**
> Visit mometrix.com/academy and enter code: 319338

Along with sleep, other aspects of physical health are important in preparing for a test. Good nutrition is vital for good brain function. Sugary foods and drinks may give a burst of energy but this burst is followed by a crash, both physically and emotionally. Instead, fuel your body with protein and vitamin-rich foods.

Also, drink plenty of water. Dehydration can lead to headaches and exhaustion, especially if your brain is already under stress from the rigors of the test. Particularly if your test is a long one, drink water during the breaks. And if possible, take an energy-boosting snack to eat between sections.

> **Review Video: <u>How Diet Can Affect your Mood</u>**
> Visit mometrix.com/academy and enter code: 624317

Along with sleep and diet, a third important part of physical health is exercise. Maintaining a steady workout schedule is helpful, but even taking 5-minute study breaks to walk can help get your blood pumping faster and clear your head. Exercise also releases endorphins, which contribute to a positive feeling and can help combat test anxiety.

When you nurture your physical health, you are also contributing to your mental health. If your body is healthy, your mind is much more likely to be healthy as well. So take time to rest, nourish your body with healthy food and water, and get moving as much as possible. Taking these physical steps will make you stronger and more able to take the mental steps necessary to overcome test anxiety.

> **Review Video: <u>How to Stay Healthy and Prevent Test Anxiety</u>**
> Visit mometrix.com/academy and enter code: 877894

Mental Steps for Beating Test Anxiety

Working on the mental side of test anxiety can be more challenging, but as with the physical side, there are clear steps you can take to overcome it. As mentioned earlier, test anxiety often stems from lack of preparation, so the obvious solution is to prepare for the test. Effective studying may be the most important weapon you have for beating test anxiety, but you can and should employ several other mental tools to combat fear.

First, boost your confidence by reminding yourself of past success—tests or projects that you aced. If you're putting as much effort into preparing for this test as you did for those, there's no reason you should expect to fail here. Work hard to prepare; then trust your preparation.

Second, surround yourself with encouraging people. It can be helpful to find a study group, but be sure that the people you're around will encourage a positive attitude. If you spend time with others who are anxious or cynical, this will only contribute to your own anxiety. Look for others who are motivated to study hard from a desire to succeed, not from a fear of failure.

Third, reward yourself. A test is physically and mentally tiring, even without anxiety, and it can be helpful to have something to look forward to. Plan an activity following the test, regardless of the outcome, such as going to a movie or getting ice cream.

When you are taking the test, if you find yourself beginning to feel anxious, remind yourself that you know the material. Visualize successfully completing the test. Then take a few deep, relaxing breaths and return to it. Work through the questions carefully but with confidence, knowing that you are capable of succeeding.

Developing a healthy mental approach to test taking will also aid in other areas of life. Test anxiety affects more than just the actual test—it can be damaging to your mental health and even contribute to depression. It's important to beat test anxiety before it becomes a problem for more than testing.

Review Video: <u>Test Anxiety and Depression</u>
Visit mometrix.com/academy and enter code: 904704

Study Strategy

Being prepared for the test is necessary to combat anxiety, but what does being prepared look like? You may study for hours on end and still not feel prepared. What you need is a strategy for test prep. The next few pages outline our recommended steps to help you plan out and conquer the challenge of preparation.

STEP 1: SCOPE OUT THE TEST

Learn everything you can about the format (multiple choice, essay, etc.) and what will be on the test. Gather any study materials, course outlines, or sample exams that may be available. Not only will this help you to prepare, but knowing what to expect can help to alleviate test anxiety.

STEP 2: MAP OUT THE MATERIAL

Look through the textbook or study guide and make note of how many chapters or sections it has. Then divide these over the time you have. For example, if a book has 15 chapters and you have five days to study, you need to cover three chapters each day. Even better, if you have the time, leave an extra day at the end for overall review after you have gone through the material in depth.

If time is limited, you may need to prioritize the material. Look through it and make note of which sections you think you already have a good grasp on, and which need review. While you are studying, skim quickly through the familiar sections and take more time on the challenging parts. Write out your plan so you don't get lost as you go. Having a written plan also helps you feel more in control of the study, so anxiety is less likely to arise from feeling overwhelmed at the amount to cover.

STEP 3: GATHER YOUR TOOLS

Decide what study method works best for you. Do you prefer to highlight in the book as you study and then go back over the highlighted portions? Or do you type out notes of the important information? Or is it helpful to make flashcards that you can carry with you? Assemble the pens, index cards, highlighters, post-it notes, and any other materials you may need so you won't be distracted by getting up to find things while you study.

If you're having a hard time retaining the information or organizing your notes, experiment with different methods. For example, try color-coding by subject with colored pens, highlighters, or post-it notes. If you learn better by hearing, try recording yourself reading your notes so you can listen while in the car, working out, or simply sitting at your desk. Ask a friend to quiz you from your flashcards, or try teaching someone the material to solidify it in your mind.

STEP 4: CREATE YOUR ENVIRONMENT

It's important to avoid distractions while you study. This includes both the obvious distractions like visitors and the subtle distractions like an uncomfortable chair (or a too-comfortable couch that makes you want to fall asleep). Set up the best study environment possible: good lighting and a comfortable work area. If background music helps you focus, you may want to turn it on, but otherwise keep the room quiet. If you are using a computer to take notes, be sure you don't have any other windows open, especially applications like social media, games, or anything else that could distract you. Silence your phone and turn off notifications. Be sure to keep water close by so you stay hydrated while you study (but avoid unhealthy drinks and snacks).

Also, take into account the best time of day to study. Are you freshest first thing in the morning? Try to set aside some time then to work through the material. Is your mind clearer in the afternoon or evening? Schedule your study session then. Another method is to study at the same time of day that you will take the test, so that your brain gets used to working on the material at that time and will be ready to focus at test time.

STEP 5: STUDY!

Once you have done all the study preparation, it's time to settle into the actual studying. Sit down, take a few moments to settle your mind so you can focus, and begin to follow your study plan. Don't give in to distractions or let yourself procrastinate. This is your time to prepare so you'll be ready to fearlessly approach the test. Make the most of the time and stay focused.

Of course, you don't want to burn out. If you study too long you may find that you're not retaining the information very well. Take regular study breaks. For example, taking five minutes out of every hour to walk briskly, breathing deeply and swinging your arms, can help your mind stay fresh.

As you get to the end of each chapter or section, it's a good idea to do a quick review. Remind yourself of what you learned and work on any difficult parts. When you feel that you've mastered the material, move on to the next part. At the end of your study session, briefly skim through your notes again.

But while review is helpful, cramming last minute is NOT. If at all possible, work ahead so that you won't need to fit all your study into the last day. Cramming overloads your brain with more information than it can process and retain, and your tired mind may struggle to recall even previously learned information when it is overwhelmed with last-minute study. Also, the urgent nature of cramming and the stress placed on your brain contribute to anxiety. You'll be more likely to go to the test feeling unprepared and having trouble thinking clearly.

So don't cram, and don't stay up late before the test, even just to review your notes at a leisurely pace. Your brain needs rest more than it needs to go over the information again. In fact, plan to finish your studies by noon or early afternoon the day before the test. Give your brain the rest of the day to relax or focus on other things, and get a good night's sleep. Then you will be fresh for the test and better able to recall what you've studied.

STEP 6: TAKE A PRACTICE TEST

Many courses offer sample tests, either online or in the study materials. This is an excellent resource to check whether you have mastered the material, as well as to prepare for the test format and environment.

Check the test format ahead of time: the number of questions, the type (multiple choice, free response, etc.), and the time limit. Then create a plan for working through them. For example, if you have 30 minutes to take a 60-question test, your limit is 30 seconds per question. Spend less time on the questions you know well so that you can take more time on the difficult ones.

If you have time to take several practice tests, take the first one open book, with no time limit. Work through the questions at your own pace and make sure you fully understand them. Gradually work up to taking a test under test conditions: sit at a desk with all study materials put away and set a timer. Pace yourself to make sure you finish the test with time to spare and go back to check your answers if you have time.

After each test, check your answers. On the questions you missed, be sure you understand why you missed them. Did you misread the question (tests can use tricky wording)? Did you forget the information? Or was it something you hadn't learned? Go back and study any shaky areas that the practice tests reveal.

Taking these tests not only helps with your grade, but also aids in combating test anxiety. If you're already used to the test conditions, you're less likely to worry about it, and working through tests until you're scoring well gives you a confidence boost. Go through the practice tests until you feel comfortable, and then you can go into the test knowing that you're ready for it.

Test Tips

On test day, you should be confident, knowing that you've prepared well and are ready to answer the questions. But aside from preparation, there are several test day strategies you can employ to maximize your performance.

First, as stated before, get a good night's sleep the night before the test (and for several nights before that, if possible). Go into the test with a fresh, alert mind rather than staying up late to study.

Try not to change too much about your normal routine on the day of the test. It's important to eat a nutritious breakfast, but if you normally don't eat breakfast at all, consider eating just a protein bar. If you're a coffee drinker, go ahead and have your normal coffee. Just make sure you time it so that the caffeine doesn't wear off right in the middle of your test. Avoid sugary beverages, and drink enough water to stay hydrated but not so much that you need a restroom break 10 minutes into the test. If your test isn't first thing in the morning, consider going for a walk or doing a light workout before the test to get your blood flowing.

Allow yourself enough time to get ready, and leave for the test with plenty of time to spare so you won't have the anxiety of scrambling to arrive in time. Another reason to be early is to select a good seat. It's helpful to sit away from doors and windows, which can be distracting. Find a good seat, get out your supplies, and settle your mind before the test begins.

When the test begins, start by going over the instructions carefully, even if you already know what to expect. Make sure you avoid any careless mistakes by following the directions.

Then begin working through the questions, pacing yourself as you've practiced. If you're not sure on an answer, don't spend too much time on it, and don't let it shake your confidence. Either skip it and come back later, or eliminate as many wrong answers as possible and guess among the remaining ones. Don't dwell on these questions as you continue—put them out of your mind and focus on what lies ahead.

Be sure to read all of the answer choices, even if you're sure the first one is the right answer. Sometimes you'll find a better one if you keep reading. But don't second-guess yourself if you do immediately know the answer. Your gut instinct is usually right. Don't let test anxiety rob you of the information you know.

If you have time at the end of the test (and if the test format allows), go back and review your answers. Be cautious about changing any, since your first instinct tends to be correct, but make sure you didn't misread any of the questions or accidentally mark the wrong answer choice. Look over any you skipped and make an educated guess.

At the end, leave the test feeling confident. You've done your best, so don't waste time worrying about your performance or wishing you could change anything. Instead, celebrate the successful

completion of this test. And finally, use this test to learn how to deal with anxiety even better next time.

Important Qualification

Not all anxiety is created equal. If your test anxiety is causing major issues in your life beyond the classroom or testing center, or if you are experiencing troubling physical symptoms related to your anxiety, it may be a sign of a serious physiological or psychological condition. If this sounds like your situation, we strongly encourage you to seek professional help.

How to Overcome Your Fear of Math

The word *math* is enough to strike fear into most hearts. How many of us have memories of sitting through confusing lectures, wrestling over mind-numbing homework, or taking tests that still seem incomprehensible even after hours of study? Years after graduation, many still shudder at these memories.

The fact is, math is not just a classroom subject. It has real-world implications that you face every day, whether you realize it or not. This may be balancing your monthly budget, deciding how many supplies to buy for a project, or simply splitting a meal check with friends. The idea of daily confrontations with math can be so paralyzing that some develop a condition known as *math anxiety*.

But you do NOT need to be paralyzed by this anxiety! In fact, while you may have thought all your life that you're not good at math, or that your brain isn't wired to understand it, the truth is that you may have been conditioned to think this way. From your earliest school days, the way you were taught affected the way you viewed different subjects. And the way math has been taught has changed.

Several decades ago, there was a shift in American math classrooms. The focus changed from traditional problem-solving to a conceptual view of topics, de-emphasizing the importance of learning the basics and building on them. The solid foundation necessary for math progression and confidence was undermined. Math became more of a vague concept than a concrete idea. Today, it is common to think of math, not as a straightforward system, but as a mysterious, complicated method that can't be fully understood unless you're a genius.

This is why you may still have nightmares about being called on to answer a difficult problem in front of the class. Math anxiety is a very real, though unnecessary, fear.

Math anxiety may begin with a single class period. Let's say you missed a day in 6th grade math and never quite understood the concept that was taught while you were gone. Since math is cumulative, with each new concept building on past ones, this could very well affect the rest of your math career. Without that one day's knowledge, it will be difficult to understand any other concepts that link to it. Rather than realizing that you're just missing one key piece, you may begin to believe that you're simply not capable of understanding math.

This belief can change the way you approach other classes, career options, and everyday life experiences, if you become anxious at the thought that math might be required. A student who loves science may choose a different path of study upon realizing that multiple math classes will be required for a degree. An aspiring medical student may hesitate at the thought of going through the necessary math classes. For some this anxiety escalates into a more extreme state known as *math phobia*.

Math anxiety is challenging to address because it is rooted deeply and may come from a variety of causes: an embarrassing moment in class, a teacher who did not explain concepts well and contributed to a shaky foundation, or a failed test that contributed to the belief of math failure.

These causes add up over time, encouraged by society's popular view that math is hard and unpleasant. Eventually a person comes to firmly believe that he or she is simply bad at math. This belief makes it difficult to grasp new concepts or even remember old ones. Homework and test grades begin to slip, which only confirms the belief. The poor performance is not due to lack of ability but is caused by math anxiety.

Math anxiety is an emotional issue, not a lack of intelligence. But when it becomes deeply rooted, it can become more than just an emotional problem. Physical symptoms appear. Blood pressure may rise and heartbeat may quicken at the sight of a math problem – or even the thought of math! This fear leads to a mental block. When someone with math anxiety is asked to perform a calculation, even a basic problem can seem overwhelming and impossible. The emotional and physical response to the thought of math prevents the brain from working through it logically.

The more this happens, the more a person's confidence drops, and the more math anxiety is generated. This vicious cycle must be broken!

The first step in breaking the cycle is to go back to very beginning and make sure you really understand the basics of how math works and why it works. It is not enough to memorize rules for multiplication and division. If you don't know WHY these rules work, your foundation will be shaky and you will be at risk of developing a phobia. Understanding mathematical concepts not only promotes confidence and security, but allows you to build on this understanding for new concepts. Additionally, you can solve unfamiliar problems using familiar concepts and processes.

Why is it that students in other countries regularly outperform American students in math? The answer likely boils down to a couple of things: the foundation of mathematical conceptual understanding and societal perception. While students in the US are not expected to *like* or *get* math, in many other nations, students are expected not only to understand math but also to excel at it.

Changing the American view of math that leads to math anxiety is a monumental task. It requires changing the training of teachers nationwide, from kindergarten through high school, so that they learn to teach the *why* behind math and to combat the wrong math views that students may develop. It also involves changing the stigma associated with math, so that it is no longer viewed as unpleasant and incomprehensible. While these are necessary changes, they are challenging and will take time. But in the meantime, math anxiety is not irreversible—it can be faced and defeated, one person at a time.

False Beliefs

One reason math anxiety has taken such hold is that several false beliefs have been created and shared until they became widely accepted. Some of these unhelpful beliefs include the following:

There is only one way to solve a math problem. In the same way that you can choose from different driving routes and still arrive at the same house, you can solve a math problem using different methods and still find the correct answer. A person who understands the reasoning behind math calculations may be able to look at an unfamiliar concept and find the right answer, just by applying logic to the knowledge they already have. This approach may be different than what is taught in the classroom, but it is still valid. Unfortunately, even many teachers view math as a subject where the best course of action is to memorize the rule or process for each problem rather than as a place for students to exercise logic and creativity in finding a solution.

Many people don't have a mind for math. A person who has struggled due to poor teaching or math anxiety may falsely believe that he or she doesn't have the mental capacity to grasp mathematical concepts. Most of the time, this is false. Many people find that when they are relieved of their math anxiety, they have more than enough brainpower to understand math.

Men are naturally better at math than women. Even though research has shown this to be false, many young women still avoid math careers and classes because of their belief that their math abilities are inferior. Many girls have come to believe that math is a male skill and have given up trying to understand or enjoy it.

Counting aids are bad. Something like counting on your fingers or drawing out a problem to visualize it may be frowned on as childish or a crutch, but these devices can help you get a tangible understanding of a problem or a concept.

Sadly, many students buy into these ideologies at an early age. A young girl who enjoys math class may be conditioned to think that she doesn't actually have the brain for it because math is for boys, and may turn her energies to other pursuits, permanently closing the door on a wide range of opportunities. A child who finds the right answer but doesn't follow the teacher's method may believe that he is doing it wrong and isn't good at math. A student who never had a problem with math before may have a poor teacher and become confused, yet believe that the problem is because she doesn't have a mathematical mind.

Students who have bought into these erroneous beliefs quickly begin to add their own anxieties, adapting them to their own personal situations:

I'll never use this in real life. A huge number of people wrongly believe that math is irrelevant outside the classroom. By adopting this mindset, they are handicapping themselves for a life in a mathematical world, as well as limiting their career choices. When they are inevitably faced with real-world math, they are conditioning themselves to respond with anxiety.

I'm not quick enough. While timed tests and quizzes, or even simply comparing yourself with other students in the class, can lead to this belief, speed is not an indicator of skill level. A person can work very slowly yet understand at a deep level.

If I can understand it, it's too easy. People with a low view of their own abilities tend to think that if they are able to grasp a concept, it must be simple. They cannot accept the idea that they are capable of understanding math. This belief will make it harder to learn, no matter how intelligent they are.

I just can't learn this. An overwhelming number of people think this, from young children to adults, and much of the time it is simply not true. But this mindset can turn into a self-fulfilling prophecy that keeps you from exercising and growing your math ability.

The good news is, each of these myths can be debunked. For most people, they are based on emotion and psychology, NOT on actual ability! It will take time, effort, and the desire to change, but change is possible. Even if you have spent years thinking that you don't have the capability to understand math, it is not too late to uncover your true ability and find relief from the anxiety that surrounds math.

Math Strategies

It is important to have a plan of attack to combat math anxiety. There are many useful strategies for pinpointing the fears or myths and eradicating them:

Go back to the basics. For most people, math anxiety stems from a poor foundation. You may think that you have a complete understanding of addition and subtraction, or even decimals and percentages, but make absolutely sure. Learning math is different from learning other subjects. For example, when you learn history, you study various time periods and places and events. It may be important to memorize dates or find out about the lives of famous people. When you move from US history to world history, there will be some overlap, but a large amount of the information will be new. Mathematical concepts, on the other hand, are very closely linked and highly dependent on each other. It's like climbing a ladder – if a rung is missing from your understanding, it may be difficult or impossible for you to climb any higher, no matter how hard you try. So go back and make sure your math foundation is strong. This may mean taking a remedial math course, going to a tutor to work through the shaky concepts, or just going through your old homework to make sure you really understand it.

Speak the language. Math has a large vocabulary of terms and phrases unique to working problems. Sometimes these are completely new terms, and sometimes they are common words, but are used differently in a math setting. If you can't speak the language, it will be very difficult to get a thorough understanding of the concepts. It's common for students to think that they don't understand math when they simply don't understand the vocabulary. The good news is that this is fairly easy to fix. Brushing up on any terms you aren't quite sure of can help bring the rest of the concepts into focus.

Check your anxiety level. When you think about math, do you feel nervous or uncomfortable? Do you struggle with feelings of inadequacy, even on concepts that you know you've already learned? It's important to understand your specific math anxieties, and what triggers them. When you catch yourself falling back on a false belief, mentally replace it with the truth. Don't let yourself believe that you can't learn, or that struggling with a concept means you'll never understand it. Instead, remind yourself of how much you've already learned and dwell on that past success. Visualize grasping the new concept, linking it to your old knowledge, and moving on to the next challenge. Also, learn how to manage anxiety when it arises. There are many techniques for coping with the irrational fears that rise to the surface when you enter the math classroom. This may include controlled breathing, replacing negative thoughts with positive ones, or visualizing success. Anxiety interferes with your ability to concentrate and absorb information, which in turn contributes to greater anxiety. If you can learn how to regain control of your thinking, you will be better able to pay attention, make progress, and succeed!

Don't go it alone. Like any deeply ingrained belief, math anxiety is not easy to eradicate. And there is no need for you to wrestle through it on your own. It will take time, and many people find that speaking with a counselor or psychiatrist helps. They can help you develop strategies for responding to anxiety and overcoming old ideas. Additionally, it can be very helpful to take a short course or seek out a math tutor to help you find and fix the missing rungs on your ladder and make sure that you're ready to progress to the next level. You can also find a number of math aids online: courses that will teach you mental devices for figuring out problems, how to get the most out of your math classes, etc.

Check your math attitude. No matter how much you want to learn and overcome your anxiety, you'll have trouble if you still have a negative attitude toward math. If you think it's too hard, or just have general feelings of dread about math, it will be hard to learn and to break through the anxiety. Work on cultivating a positive math attitude. Remind yourself that math is not just a hurdle to be cleared, but a valuable asset. When you view math with a positive attitude, you'll be much more likely to understand and even enjoy it. This is something you must do for yourself. You may find it helpful to visit with a counselor. Your tutor, friends, and family may cheer you on in your endeavors. But your greatest asset is yourself. You are inside your own mind – tell yourself what you need to hear. Relive past victories. Remind yourself that you are capable of understanding math. Root out any false beliefs that linger and replace them with positive truths. Even if it doesn't feel true at first, it will begin to affect your thinking and pave the way for a positive, anxiety-free mindset.

Aside from these general strategies, there are a number of specific practical things you can do to begin your journey toward overcoming math anxiety. Something as simple as learning a new note-taking strategy can change the way you approach math and give you more confidence and understanding. New study techniques can also make a huge difference.

Math anxiety leads to bad habits. If it causes you to be afraid of answering a question in class, you may gravitate toward the back row. You may be embarrassed to ask for help. And you may procrastinate on assignments, which leads to rushing through them at the last moment when it's too late to get a better understanding. It's important to identify your negative behaviors and replace them with positive ones:

Prepare ahead of time. Read the lesson before you go to class. Being exposed to the topics that will be covered in class ahead of time, even if you don't understand them perfectly, is extremely helpful in increasing what you retain from the lecture. Do your homework and, if you're still shaky, go over some extra problems. The key to a solid understanding of math is practice.

Sit front and center. When you can easily see and hear, you'll understand more, and you'll avoid the distractions of other students if no one is in front of you. Plus, you're more likely to be sitting with students who are positive and engaged, rather than others with math anxiety. Let their positive math attitude rub off on you.

Ask questions in class and out. If you don't understand something, just ask. If you need a more in-depth explanation, the teacher may need to work with you outside of class, but often it's a simple concept you don't quite understand, and a single question may clear it up. If you wait, you may not be able to follow the rest of the day's lesson. For extra help, most professors have office hours outside of class when you can go over concepts one-on-one to clear up any uncertainties. Additionally, there may be a *math lab* or study session you can attend for homework help. Take advantage of this.

Review. Even if you feel that you've fully mastered a concept, review it periodically to reinforce it. Going over an old lesson has several benefits: solidifying your understanding, giving you a confidence boost, and even giving some new insights into material that you're currently learning! Don't let yourself get rusty. That can lead to problems with learning later concepts.

Teaching Tips

While the math student's mindset is the most crucial to overcoming math anxiety, it is also important for others to adjust their math attitudes. Teachers and parents have an enormous influence on how students relate to math. They can either contribute to math confidence or math anxiety.

As a parent or teacher, it is very important to convey a positive math attitude. Retelling horror stories of your own bad experience with math will contribute to a new generation of math anxiety. Even if you don't share your experiences, others will be able to sense your fears and may begin to believe them.

Even a careless comment can have a big impact, so watch for phrases like *He's not good at math* or *I never liked math*. You are a crucial role model, and your children or students will unconsciously adopt your mindset. Give them a positive example to follow. Rather than teaching them to fear the math world before they even know it, teach them about all its potential and excitement.

Work to present math as an integral, beautiful, and understandable part of life. Encourage creativity in solving problems. Watch for false beliefs and dispel them. Cross the lines between subjects: integrate history, English, and music with math. Show students how math is used every day, and how the entire world is based on mathematical principles, from the pull of gravity to the shape of seashells. Instead of letting students see math as a necessary evil, direct them to view it as an imaginative, beautiful art form – an art form that they are capable of mastering and using.

Don't give too narrow a view of math. It is more than just numbers. Yes, working problems and learning formulas is a large part of classroom math. But don't let the teaching stop there. Teach students about the everyday implications of math. Show them how nature works according to the laws of mathematics, and take them outside to make discoveries of their own. Expose them to math-related careers by inviting visiting speakers, asking students to do research and presentations, and learning students' interests and aptitudes on a personal level.

Demonstrate the importance of math. Many people see math as nothing more than a required stepping stone to their degree, a nuisance with no real usefulness. Teach students that algebra is used every day in managing their bank accounts, in following recipes, and in scheduling the day's events. Show them how learning to do geometric proofs helps them to develop logical thinking, an invaluable life skill. Let them see that math surrounds them and is integrally linked to their daily lives: that weather predictions are based on math, that math was used to design cars and other machines, etc. Most of all, give them the tools to use math to enrich their lives.

Make math as tangible as possible. Use visual aids and objects that can be touched. It is much easier to grasp a concept when you can hold it in your hands and manipulate it, rather than just listening to the lecture. Encourage math outside of the classroom. The real world is full of measuring, counting, and calculating, so let students participate in this. Keep your eyes open for numbers and patterns to discuss. Talk about how scores are calculated in sports games and how far apart plants are placed in a garden row for maximum growth. Build the mindset that math is a normal and interesting part of daily life.

Finally, find math resources that help to build a positive math attitude. There are a number of books that show math as fascinating and exciting while teaching important concepts, for example: *The Math Curse; A Wrinkle in Time; The Phantom Tollbooth;* and *Fractals, Googols and Other Mathematical Tales*. You can also find a number of online resources: math puzzles and games,

videos that show math in nature, and communities of math enthusiasts. On a local level, students can compete in a variety of math competitions with other schools or join a math club.

The student who experiences math as exciting and interesting is unlikely to suffer from math anxiety. Going through life without this handicap is an immense advantage and opens many doors that others have closed through their fear.

Self-Check

Whether you suffer from math anxiety or not, chances are that you have been exposed to some of the false beliefs mentioned above. Now is the time to check yourself for any errors you may have accepted. Do you think you're not wired for math? Or that you don't need to understand it since you're not planning on a math career? Do you think math is just too difficult for the average person?

Find the errors you've taken to heart and replace them with positive thinking. Are you capable of learning math? Yes! Can you control your anxiety? Yes! These errors will resurface from time to time, so be watchful. Don't let others with math anxiety influence you or sway your confidence. If you're having trouble with a concept, find help. Don't let it discourage you!

Create a plan of attack for defeating math anxiety and sharpening your skills. Do some research and decide if it would help you to take a class, get a tutor, or find some online resources to fine-tune your knowledge. Make the effort to get good nutrition, hydration, and sleep so that you are operating at full capacity. Remind yourself daily that you are skilled and that anxiety does not control you. Your mind is capable of so much more than you know. Give it the tools it needs to grow and thrive.

Thank You

We at Mometrix would like to extend our heartfelt thanks to you, our friend and patron, for allowing us to play a part in your journey. It is a privilege to serve people from all walks of life who are unified in their commitment to building the best future they can for themselves.

The preparation you devote to these important testing milestones may be the most valuable educational opportunity you have for making a real difference in your life. We encourage you to put your heart into it—that feeling of succeeding, overcoming, and yes, conquering will be well worth the hours you've invested.

We want to hear your story, your struggles and your successes, and if you see any opportunities for us to improve our materials so we can help others even more effectively in the future, please share that with us as well. **The team at Mometrix would be absolutely thrilled to hear from you!** So please, send us an email (support@mometrix.com) and let's stay in touch.

> **If you'd like some additional help, check out these other resources we offer for your exam:**
> **http://MometrixFlashcards.com/PERT**

Additional Bonus Material

Due to our efforts to try to keep this book to a manageable length, we've created a link that will give you access to all of your additional bonus material.

Please visit http://www.mometrix.com/bonus948/pert to access the information.

Made in the USA
Columbia, SC
03 July 2021